THE
SECOND
WAVE

SEAGULL
BOOKS
•
CELEBRATING
40 YEARS

THE INDIA LIST

RUSTOM
BHARUCHA

THE
SECOND
WAVE

REFLECTIONS ON THE PANDEMIC
THROUGH PHOTOGRAPHY,
PERFORMANCE AND
PUBLIC CULTURE

LONDON NEW YORK CALCUTTA

Seagull Books, 2022

Text © Rustom Bharucha, 2022
Photographs © Individual photographers, and/or agencies
This compilation © Seagull Books, 2022

ISBN 978 1 8030 9 075 7

British Library Cataloguing-in-Publication Data
A catalogue record for this book is available from the British Library.

Typeset by Seagull Books, Calcutta, India
Printed and bound by Hyam Enterprises, Calcutta, India

While I was writing this book in one room of my apartment on a street in central Calcutta that is usually associated with chaos and cacophony, my 94-year-old mother was in the next room, immersed in a world of deep silence. So I had to deal with two silences: the unearthly silence of the street during the long months of lockdown, and the more elusive silence of my mother. In what could be regarded as a state of post-dementia, my mother continues to be oblivious of what is going on around her. I often wonder if she has processed the pandemic at all in her inner silence. Be that as it may, she has come to represent for me some kind of still centre, a calm in the eye of the storm that rages around us. And it is for this reason that this small book on the pandemic is dedicated to her.

CONTENTS

PREFACE

In medias res: 'in the midst of things', somewhere in the middle. The choice to begin the narrative here is not stylistic but directly linked to its subject matter and time frame: the 'second wave' of the pandemic in India. I could have begun this narrative with its first manifestations in March 2020, and indeed, that was the original intention. Between May and November 2020, I had already prepared and 'performed' a video-lecture in nine episodes, titled *Theatre and the Coronavirus*, in which I had reflected on the first phase in several dimensions: the global closure of theatres; the Spanish flu pandemic (when, oddly enough, theatres and cinema halls remained open in most parts of the world); the performativity of social distancing; public assemblies which defied the threat of the coronavirus through movements like Black Lives Matter and the protest against the Citizenship Amendment Act in India; online performances; the search for an ecologically tuned architecture in a post-pandemic theatre; and, finally, a meditation on learning to live with ourselves.[1]

In retrospect, I am compelled to ask myself: How did I find the energy to put together such a vast canvas of ideas even as the pandemic was spreading? The normally cacophonous street outside my house in the heart of Calcutta had begun to resemble, in

---

1 The nine-episode video-lecture on *Theatre and the Coronavirus* produced by the International Research Centre / Interweaving Performance Cultures in Berlin can be accessed on https://bityl.co/B1Tp (this and all subsequent hyperlinks in the book were last accessed on 15 May 2022).

its eerie silence, a cemetery. Was it this silence that served as a catalyst in mobilizing my thoughts relating to the theatre? Was the video-lecture simply a way of compensating for the near absence of theatre in the public discourse of the pandemic? Whatever it was, I prepared the nine-part lecture in a remarkably short span of time, almost ironically aware that the virus may have infected my words as a writer, compelling me to write at a furious speed. In these circumstances, one priority became increasingly clear to me: I wanted to deliver the lecture in the form of a 'speech-act' recorded on video. A written text of the lecture, I assumed, would follow once the pandemic died down.

But that's not what happened. Almost a year later, around April 2021, when the country at large had let its guard down and politicians were gloating that the worst of the pandemic had miraculously passed us by, we were hit by the 'second wave'. There is no other way to describe the sheer virulence of the attack: we, as a people and nation, were hit. Now it wasn't just the silence on the street and the closure of theatres that were on my mind—now I had to cope with the omnipresence of death as so many people succumbed to the virus on an almost daily basis. With death there was also grief and mourning (or, more precisely, the inability to mourn), and some unsettling premonitions of extinction that began to haunt my dreams.

Against this existential crisis, the brutal inequities of the rich and the poor, painfully made evident in the earlier days of the pandemic, intensified with the emergence of multiple vaccines competing to monopolize the world market. While some people had access to multiple doses, the vast majority in poorer countries were yet to receive their first. Panic and insecurities about public health mounted at local, national and global levels. People lost their livelihoods in cruel circumstances. Constraints on international travel were arbitrarily imposed, often with racist implications. Human interactions became strained even as, at a micro level, one experienced inexplicably tender and intimate exchanges with neighbours and strangers. At a macro level, one was made aware of the indefatigable labour of medical practitioners and workers in the service sectors, who worked harder than ever before, day and night, risking their lives to deal with a catastrophic situation.

The following report in *India Today* on 25 June 2021 sums up the scenario around death in the 'second wave':

> By March 31, 2021, a total of 1,62,468 people had lost their lives to Covid-19 in India [...]. Two months later, on May 31, India's official Covid toll had climbed up to 3,29,100. This means that more people succumbed to the virus in two months than the entire year before that. We lost 1,66,623 people in two months to Covid-19. And, these are just deaths that are on the official record.[2]

In this article, titled 'Will We Ever Get Over the Grief of the Second Wave?', it is significant how, almost overnight, the word 'wave' had displaced the more neutral use of 'phase' in the larger discourse of the pandemic in India.

It is this 'wave' that has overwhelmed the writing of this narrative, so much so that it has come to serve as the title of this short book. Almost as soon as I started writing it, I realized that my earlier nine-episode video-lecture was another narrative altogether, that seemed to have happened a long time ago. It almost seemed to be jettisoned by the brutal impact of the 'second wave'. Wouldn't it be simple, perhaps even expedient, to bring the two narratives

---

2 Tarini Mehta, 'Will We Ever Get Over the Grief of the Second Wave?', *India Today*, 25 June 2021: available at https://bityl.co/AusH.

together? The reality is that such a synthesis could not work, because the 'second wave' radically altered my perception of the pandemic. It had a different force which compelled me to think about the most basic issues of life, death, survival and resistance at an almost elemental level. And it is this force that I have tried to address in this brief narrative, which can also be read as a document of a bleak point in time, particularly between the months of April and October 2021.

While the epicentre of the pandemic registers most powerfully for me in India—and India is the inevitable location of this narrative—I am fully aware that it is a deeply global phenomenon. In writing about India, I am also writing about the world, not so much at an empirical level but in terms of how the pandemic has the capacity to haunt humans, who have never been more together in their shared vulnerabilities even as they have been distanced and forced to remain apart. More importantly, the writing of this narrative has opened me to the larger planetary dimensions of the global crisis where the nonhuman manifestations of life have taken on a new significance, beginning with the virus itself and its infinitesimal connections with global warming, climate change and the mysterious ways in which it can jump species, from bats to humans.

Returning to the idea of the elemental, there is something compulsive and never-ending about the pandemic. In this regard, the multivalent uses of the word 'wave' are worth considering. Countering the epidemiological meaning of 'wave' as a sudden upsurge of infection which can peak alarmingly, relentlessly, and then surreptitiously decline only to peak again, I am reminded at a visceral level of the Japanese woodblock print of Hokusai's *The Great Wave*, in which a massive wave threatens to swallow up three boats foregrounded against the miniaturized stillness of Mount

Fujiyama in the background. This monumental wave, frozen in its ferocious force, is no tsunami; it could be more accurately described as a 'rogue wave' precipitated by high winds and strong currents. A tsunami, on the other hand, is 'a series of waves' caused by the 'displacement of a large volume of water' through underwater explosions (including detonations and landslides), along with volcanic eruptions and earthquakes (which had been designated as the central cause of tsunamis by the Greek philosopher Thucydides in 426 BCE).[3]

Deadly as tsunamis can be—the 2004 Indian Ocean tsunami resulted in at least 230,000 people killed or missing—they are perhaps not as deadly as the pandemic that we are living with today, not just in terms of their fewer number of casualties but also in the chastening reminder that tsunamis do not 'surge' over a long period of time. They are more or less one-time annihilations of coastal regions, with the receding waters almost scraping the skin of the ocean or sea bed with terrifying speed. In contrast, the speed of any pandemic during a 'surge' in its infections is no less incremental even though it is less visible in the way it spreads. More critically, its virulence shows no signs of disappearing as it surges again and again.

In this relentless surge, the pandemic continues to throw out its statistics of mortality, rather like a whale spitting out residues of water and fish. Scrupulously unconscious of the destruction it wreaks in our lives, it is what it does. To personify its virulence in daemonic terms, which is the reflex adopted by many politicians attempting to defeat an extraterrestrial enemy, is a bit foolish and entirely misses out on the crucial fact that the pandemic has another existence.

---

3 All information relating to 'rogue wave' and the 'tsunami' are drawn from their respective Wikipedia entries.

If its unceasing persistence fills us with terror, it is a terror that cannot be entirely separated from the onslaught of statistics, even though we self-consciously remind ourselves that human beings cannot be reduced to numbers. But as the numbers of the dead increase from hundreds to thousands to tens of thousands to millions, they strike terror in our hearts. Reformulating Hannah Arendt's fiercely intelligent construct of the 'banality of evil',[4] what we may be living with is a banality of terror. Or, formulated differently, it is the terror of banality that surrounds us via statistics, state bureaucratese camouflaging its abysmal failure of governance, and the total hollowness of words—both in media reportage and our own hopelessly inadequate WhatsApp condolences.

This book does not deal with an epidemiological, statistical, scientific or historical approach to the pandemic. There are many other useful and well-documented books that serve this purpose.[5] Nor am I writing a diary or memoir, even as there are some inscriptions of my pandemic life in this narrative.[6] My focus is

---

4 Hannah Arendt, *Eichmann in Jerusalem: A Report on the Banality of Evil* (New York: Penguin, 2006).

5 For factually dense and incisive analyses of the pandemic in relation to Indian economic, epidemiological and political realities, read The India Forum, *India and the Pandemic: The First Year* (Hyderabad: Orient Blackswan, 2021); and Sunita Narain (ed.), *The Pandemic Journal* (New Delhi: Centre for Science and Environment, 2021). A more empathetic account of how people suffered during the lockdown can be read in Harsh Mander, *Locking Down the Poor: The Pandemic and India's Moral Centre* (New Delhi: Speaking Tiger, 2020). Other perspectives with a more historical focus are available in Vinay Lal, *The Fury of Covid-19: The Politics, Histories, and Unrequited Love of the Coronavirus* (New Delhi: Macmillan, 2020); Sonia Shah, *Pandemic* (New Delhi: HarperCollins, 2020); and Chinmay Tumbe, *The Age of Pandemics 1817–1920: How They Shaped India and the World* (New Delhi: HarperCollins, 2020).

6 See, for instance, Ritu Menon, *Address Book: A Publishing Memoir in the Time of Covid* (New Delhi: Women Unlimited, 2021); and K. Satchidanandan

more on a series of critical reflections about the turbulent and tragic state of a world that seems to have gone awry. Inevitably, I am implicated in my observations—and in this regard, the narrative is deeply personal as I make no attempt to conceal my distress and rage: distress because of the intensity of suffering inflicted upon people, and rage at the different forms of political indifference to human suffering, supplemented by a precipitous collapse in public healthcare and social services. Inevitably, with such an approach that combines critique with empathy, this narrative makes no attempt to provide an objective or synoptic perspective on the 'second wave'. Even if I had the ability to do so, I am not sure that such a perspective is possible.

One of the keenest challenges I have faced in putting my thoughts together is that the 'second wave' was still with us until the final stages of writing this book. It had not passed even as it appeared to be segueing into the 'third wave' yet to strike. Now that the 'third wave' has struck and spread at an alarming rate, seeming to disappear into a state of oblivion, it has in no way delegitimized the sheer virulence of the 'second wave'. In the interstice between the second and third wave, I found no clear vantage point or Archimedean location to account for the multiple implications of the 'wave', implications that extend far beyond epidemiological considerations to encompass social, political, economic, cultural, ecological and planetary realities. At a spatial level, the pandemic continues to be here, there and everywhere, in my home and in my body (as when I tested positive for Covid, even after being vaccinated twice), and in the wider world, in hospitals, vaccination centres, streets, markets and airports. At a temporal level, it may be overwhelmingly present in particular parts of the world, and

and Nishi Chawla (eds), *Singing in the Dark: A Global Anthology of Poetry under Lockdown* (New Delhi: Vintage Books, 2020).

relatively absent in others. It exists, therefore, in an omnipresent state of volatility, at once palpable in its impact and invisible in its ambience.

As we attempt to address the pandemic's ceaseless mutations and variants, its temporality proves to be tricky, if not treacherous. To deal with this temporality, I can think of no form that is more appropriate to addressing this moment than the flexible and intimate form of the essay—or the 'long essay'. I turn to the essay because its form facilitates twists and turns in the narrative, detours and shifts in perspective from microscopic details to a wide-angle lens. I am not sure to what extent the pandemic itself has inadvertently shaped the disjunctive rhythm of one's thinking, but based on my earlier nine-episode video-lecture and this essay in three parts which is performative in its own right, I would acknowledge that writing about the pandemic is a mercurial process particularly while it is still an ongoing phenomenon. We do not have the privilege of critical hindsight to correct or to inflect what we are writing. These reflections are happening *now*, in the thick of the pandemic.

Returning to the form of the essay, I would acknowledge that I have been constantly taken by surprise during the writing process by quick reflexes and connections cutting across different contexts of critical inquiry. While these reflexes and connections may have a logic of their own, they are driven less by rational argument than by a cluster of associations and an openness to illuminations of the political unconscious and myth. Occasionally, as some of my readers have pointed out, my narrative enters an almost stream-of-consciousness mode of writing (particularly apparent in the third chapter) that I have made no attempt to regulate. In writing about the pandemic, therefore, I do not restrict myself to the specificities of its phenomenon; rather, like a catalyst, the pandemic compels me to think about other phenomena or narratives from the past that ignite within the immediacies of the present moment.

Reflecting on three themes—death, grief and mourning, and extinction—I interrogate their multivalent dynamics through specific artistic languages and disciplines. For the first chapter on death and the suffering of people during the lockdown, particularly the multitude of internal migrant labourers, I focus primarily on the evidence of photography and its ethical and legal implications. I must emphasize that I am not attempting to encapsulate a history of photography in relation to earlier epidemics or pandemics, which would require a different narrative. For the second chapter, I turn to performance, fiction and visual art to throw light on symptoms of grief, delayed mourning (or no mourning), and the different artistic representations by which grief can be spectacularized or problematized in the larger contexts of economic survival and social struggle. For the last chapter on extinction, I focus on the possibilities of rethinking the interstice between beginnings and ends by reflecting on the 'end of the world' as a trope via readings of genocide in the Mahabharata, ecocide in the nonhuman world, the museumization of mourning at the Hiroshima Peace Memorial Museum, all of which take me to the coda that engages with the act of breathing in an age of breathlessness.

Instead of spelling out here how I shift gears from one context to another, I would prefer that you share some of the surprise that I felt on discovering these connections as they came to life in the narrative. It goes without saying that in all these choices that there are also omissions and exclusions for which I seek your understanding. I am only too aware that these reflections are by no means comprehensive. Even as they are cast primarily in the language of cultural critique—and some of the critique is written in the direct mode of 'plainspeak'—they are the outcome of different moods, ranging from the ominous to the whimsical. If the book serves at all as a 'document' of the second wave, I would acknowledge that it is a personally invested document that attempts to work against the grain of reducing the pandemic to an epidemiological phenomenon or a testing ground of a priori truths drawn from the physical and social sciences. From the perspective of the humanities and the arts, I would like to believe that there are other ways in which one can learn to understand and live with the pandemic. And, in this regard, I would acknowledge an odd sense of gratitude to the pandemic as a long-overdue wake-up call to rethink and re-envision what it means to be human.

1.

Photography in the Pandemic

PREAMBLE

There are at least two reasons why I choose to begin with photography. The first is empirical, as photography has contributed to several archives of images that provide evidence of what happened during the pandemic in the public sphere—in hospitals, crematoria and burial grounds. The second is experiential, because it is through these images that I was able to access the magnitude and extremity of the pandemic from within the safe confines of my home. Through the reflections that follow in this chapter, I will juxtapose both the empirical and the experiential, calling attention to the economic, political and legal dimensions of photography at national and global levels, as well as the visceral and emotional dimensions of encountering death and suffering through photographs.

I begin with the empirical because it enables us to contextualize the actual conditions of photography during the pandemic. During the worst months of the 'second wave', when all art and cultural institutions were shut down, and there was no possibility of engaging with almost any form of cultural practice in the public domain, it was photography that remained active. Arguably hyperactive even as it remained largely invisible, photography asserted itself as a medium with little attention paid to critical reflexivity and matters relating to the politics and ethics of representation. What mattered to photographers in the field was the opportunity to record the most striking images of the pandemic in all its turbulent immediacy. Despite onerous challenges in negotiating the infected no-go zones of the public sphere, those photographers who dared to leave the safety of their homes took formidable risks with their own lives in recording some of the worst manifestations of disease and death.

Confined within my home through the 'second wave', I am grateful to these photographers for making me *see* what was happening in my city and elsewhere. An obvious reason why photography was able to defy the constraints on mobility imposed by the pandemic can be linked to its relative absence of a technological apparatus beyond a camera. Despite the introduction of new and sophisticated technologies like drones, which were used for panoramic aerial shots of crematoria in the pandemic, it was the hand-held camera or phone that captured most of the images. One is not claiming here any particular 'innocence' or 'neutrality' in the apparatus of the camera, still less any illusion that it facilitates a sense of 'freedom' in representing the pandemic. It could well be that the seemingly modest and light apparatus of the camera, far from being in the control of the photographers, was, in fact, controlling the choices of the images being made with seeming spontaneity and split-second reflexes. What cannot be denied, however, is that the camera facilitated the recording of the pandemic with lightning speed, almost suggesting that the volatility of the pandemic had finally met its match in the temporality of photography.

Along with professional photographers, one needs to keep in mind the non-specialists, who are as capable of recording a memorable image as any professional. The photographs of these non-specialists, I should acknowledge, were also part of my daily viewing of the pandemic across the social networks. Call it accident or chance, or a freak illumination of the real. The contingencies and ephemera of life, the moment that passes with the blink of an eye, lend themselves to being photographed with a synergy that is not readily found in those arts that take a long time to be produced, notably theatre, cinema, painting, sculpture and fiction, all of which also require the training of specialized skills. Likewise, art photography or photojournalism are outcomes of carefully honed skills and experience. Nonetheless, the 'expertise' of non-professional photographers has been legitimized in recent years with the ubiquity of digital photography, where the camera has been substituted by the smartphone, enabling people at large to take images of just about anything that catches their attention—from banal images of everyday landscapes in which 'selfies' are inscribed to the most searing scenes of crime in public spaces, as demonstrated, for instance, in racist police brutality or the lynching of minorities in communal scenarios.

The smartphone has also been used to capture moments of death, and, in some cases, to record or livestream funeral services or cremation ceremonies for family and friends either elsewhere in the same city or abroad. At one level, this virtualization of the real has enabled individuals and entire families to watch the last rites for a loved one in a faraway place; at another level, it has deepened feelings of alienation and numbness. For me, the struggle to write about photography in the pandemic is directly related to such ambivalence for which there is no precedent in our everyday lives. As the following pages will reveal, I am conflicted about the contradictory conditions and effects of photography. On the one hand, I am alerted to how images are owned, censored and circulated in states of emergency; on the other, I am keenly aware of how the actual emotional experience of engaging with the moment of death in a particular photograph can result in a breaking point, where public grief collapses into an inexplicable sense of personal loss.

Instead of attempting to provide an overview of photography in the pandemic, or to consider the vast image archive that now exists, I choose to focus on three photographs. While images are not known to 'speak', I would acknowledge that these images have compelled me to speak to them and through their visual components. Occasionally, I have attempted to argue against what they may be attempting to 'say', keeping in mind that these three images may be regarded as 'iconic shots'. They are perhaps among the most circulated and the ones most likely to be remembered; perhaps, also for that very reason, they are the most fraught with contested meanings. If I turn to these images, it is not because I believe that they exemplify a political attitude of resistance to the greed of neoliberal capitalism and private ownership that dominates the archives of photography. Nor do I believe that they are free of problems relating to sensationalism or voyeurism—they are certainly not working within the framework of political correctness. Nor can they be regarded as 'definitive' (insofar as any photograph can be essentialized as a final statement of an event or a catastrophe). I have selected these images because they resonate with an unusual 'force'—both an 'evidential force'[1] in which Roland Barthes locates the relationship of a photograph to the

---

1 Roland Barthes, *Camera Lucida: Reflections on Photography* (Richard Howard trans.) (New York: Hill and Wang, 1981), p. 89.

event recorded as well as a mythical force that resists theorization at fundamental levels.

The evidence of photography has been problematized over the years even as it continues to be a tenacious point of reference. In earlier writings by Barthes and Susan Sontag, we encounter an almost common-sense understanding of a photograph's evidence in terms of the prior existence of a person or event being recorded. Emphasizing that a photograph has the capacity to 'attest that what I see has indeed existed', Barthes qualifies that while it may deceive 'as to the meaning of the thing [being photographed]', it can never lie as to its 'existence'.[2] In a similar register, Susan Sontag in On Photography argues that 'Photographs furnish evidence [...]. The picture may distort; but there is always a presumption that something exists, or did exist, which is like what's in the picture.'[3] Against these normative positions relating to photography, Allan Sekula debunks the readymade evidence of photography, arguing that, 'The only "objective" truth that photography offers is the assertion that somebody or some thing [for example, an automated camera] was somewhere and took a picture. Everything else, everything beyond, the imprinting of a trace, is up for grabs.'[4]

Without entering the theoretical intricacies of this debate at this point, I would simply emphasize that the photographs represented in this chapter do provide evidence of events relating to the pandemic. It would be disingenuous to claim that what they represent did not 'exist' or that they were entirely 'made up'. One

2 Barthes, Camera Lucida, pp. 82, 87.

3 Susan Sontag, On Photography (New York: Anchor Books Doubleday, 1977), p. 5.

4 Allan Sekula, 'Dismantling Modernism, Reinventing Documentary (Notes on the Politics of Representation)', Massachusetts Review 19(4) (Winter 1978): 859–83; here, p. 863.

can question their modes of representation and specific tonalities in relation to their framing, grain and texture, but it would be a severe disservice to the photographers concerned to undermine their attempt to capture moments of an exceptionally harsh reality. What is needed is a contextualization of these images within the particularities of their locations, along with an acknowledgement that within some discursive frameworks, such as the law, these images are not likely to provide 'forensic evidence' for the larger purposes of justice. I will return to the legal protocols of determining evidence in the last section of this chapter.

For the moment, what needs to be highlighted is that people were dying around me as I encountered these photographs for the first time. How these images are likely to resonate at a later point in time, I am not sure. But I cannot entirely separate the aesthetics of these images from the intensities of the historical moment. It is for this reason that I begin my narrative with these images because they enable us to think about realities that pervaded life in the darkest moment of multiple deaths, even as we may not have witnessed any of these realities first-hand or, as the saying goes, in flesh and blood. The writing that follows, therefore, can be read as a critical engagement with seeing through the pandemic, darkly. Hopefully, some glimmers of light will enter my words in and through the darkness.

HOSPITAL

To begin with: chaos. In an environment that is supposed to be ordered and calm but where the air itself is being asphyxiated, we see two men sharing a hospital bed, oxygen masks and plastic pouches on their noses and mouths. They are in the casualty ward of Lok Nayak Jai Prakash Hospital, New Delhi, during the 'second wave', when hospital beds were hard to find. Many people died waiting to receive oxygen in their homes or because their oxygen supply was cut off by the hospital as it faced a shortage.[5] Documenting the sheer scale of these disasters, there are other photographs showing long lines of ambulances waiting to enter hospital premises, and equally long lines of empty oxygen cylinders waiting to be filled.

In these dire circumstances, it would seem that the two nameless men sharing the hospital bed were the lucky ones who managed to get admitted and receive oxygen support. For how long, we cannot say. Nor do we know if they survived. People sharing beds in a hospital are not a new phenomenon in India. Indeed, it

---

5 The most rigorous and accountable reportage of the oxygen crisis has been covered in *The Caravan*—see, for instance, Chahat Rana, 'Citizens Collect Data as Government Obscures Oxygen Shortage Deaths Based on Technicalities', *The Caravan*, 6 August 2021: available at https://bityl.co/Ausq. Crucial events covered in Rana's article can be read in Anonna Dutt, '20 Patients Die at Delhi's Jaipur Golden Hospital Due to Oxygen Shortage', *The Hindustan Times*, 24 April 2021: available at https://bityl.co/Ausz; *The Hindu*, 'Oxygen Shortage: 12 Lives Lost in Delhi's Batra Hospital', 1 May 2021: available at https://bityl.co/Aut7. From Rana's article, we learn how the State has attempted to camouflage the number of deaths resulting from the oxygen crisis by claiming that the necessary 'data' has not been submitted by the hospitals. This is further complicated by the fact that while the pro forma for all Covid-19 deaths, as submitted to the Indian Council of Medical Research, included 'death due to COVID-19 and death due to COVID-19 and co-morbidities', there was no specific provision for deaths caused by oxygen shortage. As yet, there is no database for those patients who died at home.

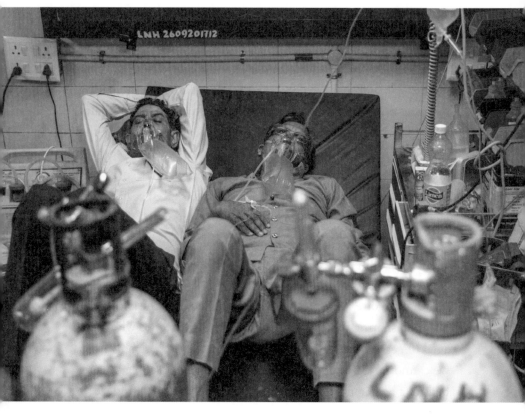

PHOTOGRAPH BY DANISH SIDDIQUI

is regular practice in most public hospitals which are, invariably, overcrowded and short of basic medical infrastructure. The most terrifying image that highlights this phenomenon is Deepa Dhanraj's documentary film *Something Like a War* (1991), a chilling exposure of the reproductive rights—or, more precisely, the annihilation of such rights—of women in India through the government family-planning programme, and its coerced sterilizations using experimental techniques. In the opening sequence, we see a number of women in quick succession being made to lie down on a bed, after which the 'miracle-doctor', who is credited with thousands of laparoscopic sterilizations, jabs them and ties their fallopian tubes in 'an economic and safe procedure'. Seconds later, the women, in a state of shock, and in acute pain, are removed from the bed and made to lie en masse on the floor.

Arguably, the pandemic was also 'something like a war'. While the government would like to believe that it was waging a war against the virus, the reality was that it was waging a war against ordinary people—a war in which ordinary people were allowed to die through systematic neglect and indifference. One is reminded here of Jacques Derrida's powerful questions: 'Does killing necessarily mean "putting to death"? Isn't it also "letting die"? Isn't "letting die", "not wanting to know that one is letting others die" also be part of a "more or less" conscious and deliberate terrorist strategy?'[6] Photographer Danish Siddiqui's image of the two men sharing the hospital bed captures this sense of unacknowledged 'terror' even as it represents the larger health crisis in India.[7]

---

6 Jacques Derrida, 'Autoimmunity: Real and Symbolic Suicides' in Giovanna Borradori (ed.), *Philosophy in a Time of Terror: Dialogues with Jürgen Habermas and Jacques Derrida* (Chicago: University of Chicago Press, 2003), p. 116.
7 At the best of times, the national budget for health in India is a mere 1.25 per cent of the GDP. But Arundhati Roy points out that this official figure is

Shortly after taking this photograph, on 16 July 2021, Siddiqui, a Pulitzer Prize–winning photographer attached to Reuters and known for his coverage of the Rohingya refugees, was caught in the crossfire between Afghan government forces and the Taliban. While being treated for his wounds, he was killed by the Taliban, his body mutilated. In contrast to his tragic end in a war zone, his photograph of the two men in hospital is, in the best tradition of photojournalism, almost emphatically matter-of-fact.[8] While his image is not accompanied by any commentary or an extended footnote, it provokes discussion around basic issues surrounding life and death. For me, there is critical value both in the content of the photograph, and in the debate that it stimulates around the Indian government's lack of public healthcare.

Returning to the image, the casualty ward of the hospital looks like a makeshift space—there is no sheet on the bed, no pillow, and the shiny rexine-upholstered hospital bed which is raised at the top seems so narrow, if not scrunched, that the two men have to lie on their backs with their knees raised uncomfortably. Behind the bed one sees white bathroom tiles on the wall. Pipes and a tangle of wires seem to proliferate in every nook and corner. Foregrounded at the bottom of the image are the tops of two dis-coloured oxygen cylinders with the hospital initials 'LNH' painted clumsily on one of their surfaces. The same initials with a long series of numbers are also painted in minuscule letters on what appears to be a board or a screen behind the two men. In Indian public institutions, such inscriptions are visible on chairs, tables,

---

inflated, and that the Indian government could in fact be spending an abysmal 0.34 per cent—for a nation which has nearly 1.4 billion people. See '"We Are Witnessing a Crime against Humanity": Arundhati Roy on India's Covid Catastrophe', *The Guardian*, 28 April 2021: available at https://bityl.co/AutE.
8 As the book goes to press, we learn that Siddiqui has won a second Pulitzer Prize, posthumously, for his images of Covid's toll in India, along with Adnan Abidi, whose photography will be examined in the following section.

desks, cupboards and computers, and are painted on to catalogue 'institutional property'.

The image of the casualty ward in all its messy anonymity exemplifies what has been described—and disparaged—by Barthes as the 'studium', encompassing the generality of a particular scene with a unified composition and subject matter. Barthes describes such images as 'unary' insofar as they represent 'a unified and self-contained whole', which is ordered in such a 'comprehensible' way that the 'meaning can be taken in at a glance'.[9] For Barthes, this is the stuff of news photographs which fail to interest him in their absence of any detail or disturbance which he associates with the much-valorized 'punctum'. Without attempting to euphemize his distaste for 'emergency reportage', Barthes confesses: 'I tear up my notes as soon as I write them. What—nothing to say about death, suicide, wounds, accidents? No, nothing to say about these photographs in which I see surgeon's gowns, bodies lying on the ground, broken glass, etc.' He then adds with what could be read as anguish or angst or affectation, or a combination of all three: 'Oh, if there were only a look, a subject's look, if only someone in the photograph were looking at me! For the Photograph has this power [. . .] of *looking me straight in the eye*.'[10]

Clearly, there is no such possibility in Siddiqui's photo where the two men stare outwards, the younger man with his arms stretched behind his head, eyes closed, the bespectacled older man looking upwards, his head slightly askew, his expression helpless. Neither of them looks at the camera. It is we who have to look at the men. We cannot expect, as Barthes yearns for the subject's look, for them to look at us.

---

9 Barthes, *Camera Lucida*, p. 41. See also annotation of 'studium' in 'Roland Barthes: Camera Lucida — Lecture 10', 28 March 2017, in the blog titled *Photography Theory* by Nickie Marland: available at https://bityl.co./AutH.
10 Barthes, *Camera Lucida*, p. 111, for both citations.

What matters in the final analysis is that it is Siddiqui who, with his photographer's eye and social consciousness, looks at them, takes in their condition and commits himself to an image worth recording. For me it is this commitment to look, to pause and to click the camera, that makes the photograph's studium come alive in its orchestrated chaos. At a broader level, the image testifies to the collapse of the Indian health system, where oxygen was either in short supply or not available for thousands of civilians who choked to death. Whether this can be described as a 'dereliction of public duty' or as 'a crime against humanity',[11] as Arundhati Roy emphasizes, would depend at one level on the definition of oxygen as a life-resource, and not just another medication—a resource that one would expect to find in any hospital, especially during a state of emergency. To learn of parents, brothers or sisters, husbands or wives, partners or friends, or unknown civilians, choking to death because oxygen was not available remains for me one of the most oppressive memories of the 'second wave', all the more unforgiveable as it continues to be vehemently denied by the government. Against the official defence that hospitals have no records of oxygen shortage—in all candour, can one expect such acknowledgements of negligence to exist?—one needs to accept the cruel but chastening fact that many individuals might have lived if oxygen had been available.

The hospital, as Siddiqui memorializes it through his altogether matter-of-fact yet chilling photograph, is a double-edged phenomenon: both a temporary refuge and a repository of chaos, both a site of privilege and an official space of random care or an absence of care. In its strained resources for protecting life, it also sustains the imminence of death.

---

11 Roy, 'We Are Witnessing a Crime against Humanity'.

CREMATORIA

The second image is a lot more dramatic, almost elemental—a man runs through a crematorium, funeral pyres blazing on either side. With his body bent, his face looking to the ground, his hands raised to his head almost in supplication, the man seems to be not just running but *fleeing* the tongues of flame that almost surround him. 'Viral apocalypse' and 'Covid hell' are some of the expressions that have been used as captions in the international media to describe this image, among other images of the crematoria, that marked the deadly inauguration of India's 'second wave'.[12]

Both words—'apocalypse' and 'hell'—suggest the end of the world through catastrophic destruction. In a politically correct reflex, I am aware how words like 'apocalypse' and 'hell' can play into an Orientalist narrative of the burning ghats—cremation grounds that have been exoticized in the colonial archive with a relish for the macabre and grotesque. In actuality, the *shmashana* ('cremation ground') is where dead bodies are cremated following prescribed rituals. Then the ashes are immersed in a river or water body, to signify the soul of the deceased being freed from its mortal coils to enter the state of a possible liberation or *moksha*.

But this is, perhaps, too normative a reading of what happened in India. Such was the influx of bodies in the cremation grounds at the very start of the 'second wave' that there were serpentine queues, often kilometres long, outside them. The shortage of wood was so acute that multiple bodies had often to be placed on the same pyre; some bodies were not completely burned. While *shmashanas* at the best of times are rarely experienced as repositories of peace and quiet, quite unlike the sanitized and meticulously ordered cemeteries of

---

12 Philip Sherwell, 'Modi Leads India into Viral Apocalypse', *The Australian*, 25 April 2021: available at https://bityl.co/AutY; Hannah Ellis-Petersen, '"The System Has Collapsed": India's Descent into Covid Hell', *The Guardian*, 21 April 2021: available at https://bityl.co/Autd.

PHOTOGRAPH BY ADNAN ABIDI

the West, they have a spiritual corporeality that is held together by what may be described as a complex order within chaos.

With the pandemic, however, this order-in-chaos exploded into a state of *pandemonium*—a word attributed to Milton in his evocation of the capital of Hell in *Paradise Lost*, Satan's open house to all demons. This may seem a far cry from the human tragedy in India where thousands of people, grieving for their lost ones, had to face a total breakdown of funerary rites and protocols, extending to the humiliation of paying bribes—often grossly unaffordable sums—to touts to get bodies burned on time. Most painfully, some individuals had to leave the cremation ground without the obligatory ashes of the deceased. For me, this is the ultimate violation of a Hindu funerary ritual, denying any acceptance that the dead have been freed from pain and suffering, disrupting every possibility of peace and any semblance of human dignity.

Returning to the image of the man fleeing the cremation ground. The first association that comes to my mind is the end of the war in Mahabharata and its larger resonances of death, destruction and extinction. Needless to say, I am not the only person thinking about the Mahabharata in the larger context of the pandemic. No less prominent a personality than Narendra Modi had invoked the epic at the very outset of the pandemic, on 25 March 2020, a day after he announced a three-week national lockdown with the termination of road, rail and air services, giving the citizens of India exactly four hours to work out their modes of survival. In his own constituency of Varanasi, he declared with his inimitable bombast: 'The Mahabharata war was won in 18 days, this war [against Covid that] the whole country is fighting against [. . .] will take 21 days.'[13] Famous last words? Or the beginning of

---

13 Quoted in 'Coronavirus: Aim Is to Win the War against COVID-19 in 21 Days, Says Narendra Modi', *The Hindu*, 25 March 2020: available at: https://bityl.co/AutQ.

new forms of denialism as the war against the coronavirus in India has extended far beyond 21 days to more than 21 months with no end in sight?

Rejecting the epistemology of 'war' in a triumphalist sense, and with no belief that the virus can be 'defeated', I am nonetheless reminded at a metaphorical level of a Mahabharata that continues to be fought in our times. When I look at the lone figure of the man fleeing the cremation ground, I do not see any semblance of victory but, rather, the most abject representation of survival. I see 'bare life'[14] reduced to its most rudimentary essentials. In his wiry musculature and kinetic desperation, it seems as if the man is running out of the framework of the photograph into a world that won't allow him to stop. In his anonymity, he is akin to one of the millions of unknown soldiers who fought and died in the Mahabharata war—they are never named and about them no stories are told. For all its omniscience and somewhat smug self-estimation—that what is not found in the Mahabharata is not likely to be found anywhere else—the epic is not without its gaps and exclusions. There is, for instance, no reference to a pandemic in its eighteen books, and only passing references to drought.

Returning to the figure of the Unknown Soldier, it is worth recalling that Yudhishthira, eldest of the Pandavas, testifies that one billion, six hundred and sixty million, and twenty thousand men died in the war.[15] Yet another statistic, it could be argued, which is neither fleshed out nor duly respected. In contrast, the deaths of the privileged sons of the protagonists—the Pandavas and the Kauravas—are lamented and their bodies cremated with all ritual solemnity. Recontextualizing the words of Judith Butler

---

14 Giorgio Agamben, *Homo Sacer: Sovereign Power and Bare Life* (Daniel Heller-Roazen trans.) (Stanford: Stanford University Press, 1998).

15 This figure is mentioned by Yudhishthira to Dhritarashtra in *Stri Parva*, the eleventh of eighteen books in the Mahabharata.

in the larger context of *Frames of War: When Is Life Grievable?* (2019), one could say that the privileged characters of the Mahabharata are worth grieving for, but the unknown soldiers constitute the 'ungrievable', not because they are implicitly othered but because, in the final analysis, they do not really matter.[16]

Is the lone man in the photograph, cowering from our gaze, one such 'ungrievable' individual? He may or may not survive his flight. But what is he running away from? The smoke and the stench of dead bodies? Or some kind of premonition about the end of the world? When we place this image against other photographs of cremation grounds shot by the same photographer—Adnan Abidi, part of the same Reuters team as Danish Siddiqui—we witness more surreal images of mourning.

One particularly memorable one is that of a middle-aged Indian woman dressed in a sari but with her face encased in a plastic mask and shield. This hybrid juxtaposition of a human body and plastic face makes her look humanoid. She, the sole mourner, stands beside an empty hospital trolley on which her dead husband had been brought to the cremation ground. In the background, there are three funeral pyres, surrounded by bricks, stones and debris. Against them, the woman stands still, her face lifted slightly, her hands clasped around an object that remains undecipherable. She appears to be grieving even as it is hard to see her grief behind the mask and shield. Would she be representative of Gandhari, the mother of the hundred Kaurava brothers, who witnesses and laments all her sons being slaughtered in the battleground of Kurukshetra? In the sari-clad, masked and shielded figure of the sole female mourner, Abidi makes us see how difficult it is to mourn in our times. And it is this evidence that makes us question 'mourning' itself.

---

16 Judith Butler, *Frames of War: When Is Life Grievable?* (London: Verso, 2010).

PHOTOGRAPH BY RITESH SHUKLA

GANGA

In contrast to the omnipresence of fire in the crematoria images, the third image focuses on what appears to be an expanse of water—an expanse that almost fills the length and breadth of the photograph, a massive, muddy river with eddying currents, covered with rectangular patches of saffron-coloured cloth, their four edges held up by sticks. Examined more closely, it becomes somewhat clearer that these pieces of cloth are embedded in the banks of a river, where the slush of wet earth appears to be fluid. Divested of a context, it would be hard to figure out what so many pieces of cloth are doing on the riverbank. They seem to be limitless in number. This generic understanding of the overall image—the studium—only begins to make sense when one's eye turns to the left-hand bottom corner where we see four men on a drier part of the riverbank, carrying a funeral bier layered with marigolds. This sliver of an image showing the men moving forwards in one direction acts like a punctum, a detail that sets the larger image of the riverbank and its saffron contents into perspective through the principle of juxtaposition.

The punctum does not necessarily have to 'sting' or 'wound' or 'prick', even as these words are favoured by Barthes. It can also appear unobtrusively, almost invisibly. In this particular case, photographer Ritesh Shukla has consciously framed the photograph with the minuscule funeral procession set against the vast expanse of the riverbank. In other instances of the punctum, a photographer may not be aware of the detail that seizes the viewer's eye insofar as it remains 'undetectable' to the photographer.[17]

---

17 Barthes has many different associations for the 'punctum'. He sees it as 'an element which rises from the scene [of the photograph], shoots out of it like an arrow, and pierces me. A Latin word [punctum] exists to designate this wound, this prick, this mark made by a pointed instrument' (Camera Lucida, p. 26). Later, he describes the punctum as 'sting, speck, cut, little hole—and also a cast of the dice' (p. 27).

Paradoxically, the punctum is always an 'addition' endowed with a 'private meaning'—'it is what I add to the photograph and *what is nonetheless already there*.'[18]

Shukla's photograph may be somewhat too self-consciously constructed to meet the subtle demands of Barthes' punctum, but this does not mean that the image has been set up. The funeral procession seems to have passed by when he least expected it, and it is this flash of everyday life which illuminates the terrifying reality—that the saffron patches on the riverbank are in fact dead bodies swathed in cloth. At no point does one see even the barest outline of a body part; only the colour saffron and the shifting shapes of the cloth that suggest the remains of the dead.

In its overall impact, there is an eerie beauty to the photograph, which inevitably compels one to question the problematic dynamics of aesthetics in representing death. On one side of Shukla's photographic gaze is the expanse of the riverbank embedded with dead bodies. On the other side, as revealed in his accompanying photographs, are a multitude of shallow graves of Covid-19 victims, scattered all along the upper banks of the river. Like the corpses embedded in wet mud, these graves are also covered with saffron cloth but very loosely, as if the wind and rain have attempted to exhume the bodies from the sandy earth.

In this sense, they are the opposite of documentary photographer Susan Meiselas' 'mass grave exhumations' of dead bodies in Kurdistan, which had to be dug up with the utmost care and vigilance in order to arrive at an accurate testimony of bones, mutilations and identities.[19] As Allan Sekula praises Meiselas'

---

18 Barthes, *Camera Lucida*, p. 55.

19 These 'exhumations' of dead bodies as represented in Susan Meiselas' *Kurdistan: In the Shadow of History* (1997) are analysed by Allan Sekula in 'Photography and the Limits of National Identity', *Grey Room* 55 (2014): 28–33; available at https://bityl.co/BIFN.

'radical nominalism' in her relentless quest to give each dead body its due weight and consideration, he makes us see how her search for 'forensic evidence' has succeeded in unearthing a 'buried archive' by which another history of the much-demonized Kurd people can be resurrected.[20] In contrast, there is no such exhumation of the dead on the sandy banks of the Ganga—following the whims of nature, they are exhumed of their own accord. Buried in haste, these bodies are exposed from their graves and remain unnamed, anonymous, in their pitiful absence of dignity, naked and decomposed.

Returning to the problematic of photography's aesthetics in the larger context of exhumations, it is useful to keep in mind Meiselas' statement: 'When you are working with evidence—say when you're digging up grave sites—you don't want people to think it is conceptual art, an installation, or that it's just invented.'[21] This kind of exactitude in testifying to the 'evidence' of bodies is not to be found in Shukla's more rarefied images of mass death. In both sets of his photographs of bodies on the lower and upper parts of the riverbank, the perspective is aerial—the camera attempts to capture the panorama of the graves from a height, without zeroing in on a close-up.

Divested of specificity, the images radiate an oddly abstract sense of design, almost like environmental installations, that compel one to recall Walter Benjamin's unfailingly prescient words:

the camera is now incapable of photographing a tenement or a rubbish heap without transfiguring it. Not to mention a river dam or an electric cable factory: in front of these,

---

20 Sekula, 'Photography and the Limits of National Identity', p. 32.
21 Quoted in Liz Jobey, 'Photographer Susan Meiselas: "Why Am I Making This Picture?"', *The Guardian*, 12 December 2008: available at https://bityl.co/Autx

photography can only say, 'How beautiful.' [. . .] It has succeeded in turning abject poverty itself, by handling it in a modish, technically perfect way into an object of enjoyment.[22]

Benjamin's words can be transferred meaningfully to address the transfiguration of corpses in Shukla's images, where dead bodies are camouflaged by patches of saffron cloth. In their strangely enigmatic presence, one is almost tempted to say, 'How beautiful.'

Without any captions to explain Shukla's undeniably arresting images, it would be hard to imagine that they were shot on the banks of the Ganga on 20 May 2021 in Shringverpur, northwest of Allahabad, Uttar Pradesh. In other words, they were shot on hallowed ground at that critical point in time when thousands of people were dying of Covid-19 in India, not just in the cities but in rural areas as well. The Ganga became the only affordable dumping site for poor families unable to afford a regular cremation. In addition to this abject poverty, one should not ignore that bodies infected by the virus were doubly stigmatized—first, as corpses in their own right, and additionally, as corpses in which the virus still lurked. In this regard, it would be wrong to assume that the stigma of the coronavirus existed only in the cities; reinforced by fear and an ignorance of the basic facts relating to infection and contagion, it was equally tenacious in rural areas. Given the dominant realities of poverty, ignorance and fear, a quick disposal of dead bodies in the river was the most expedient way of preventing the disease from spreading.

---

22 This much-quoted insight by Walter Benjamin was first made in a lecture in 1934 at the Institute for the Study of Fascism in Paris (quoted by Sontag in *On Photography*, p. 107). A different translation can be found in Walter Benjamin, 'The Author as Producer' in *Reflections: Essays, Aphorisms, Autobiographical Writings* (Edmund Jephcott trans., Peter Demetz ed.) (New York: Schocken Books, 1986), p. 230.

As one begins to take in the cruel gravity of these facts, the photographs of dead bodies on the banks of the Ganga take on a more unsettling aura, not least because they etherealize the materiality of the dead. One should keep in mind that the dead bodies themselves in all their disintegrating corporeality are not likely to remain embedded in the riverbanks. At some point, they are bound to putrefy and decay. Rarely has death been more massively demeaned in the Indian subcontinent as it has during the pandemic.

CENSORSHIP

How are photographs of the pandemic being viewed these days? I do not mean at a hermeneutic or affective level, but in terms of their access. Rarely do we see photographs today in all their materiality, still less we do have an opportunity to touch them as objects. In the ubiquitous digitality of our times, most photographs appear as images on our computer screens or smartphones—these are the new apertures, rectangular and oblong, which enable us to access the pandemic in all its terrifying visuality. If the rectangular screen of the computer tends to replicate the proscenium, in which we see images of the pandemic framed for our spectatorship, the oblong shape of the smartphone becomes an extension of the hand—through the sensation of touch, it provides an even more intimate encounter with hospitals, crematoria and dead bodies. Significantly, even as we have been deprived of sensory contact during the pandemic in the absence of person-to-person interactions, our almost obsessive fixation with accessing information via the smartphone has enhanced our connection with 'haptic technology—kinaesthetic communication or 3D touch'.[23]

---

23 See the Wikipedia entry on Haptic Technology.

So omnipresent is this tactile access to the real that it has rendered almost redundant the older modes of receiving the 'news of the day' via newspapers. In the Indian scenario, newspapers are becoming thinner and thinner, both in their size and content. This could be related to the fact that they are unable to compete with television and the digital media in terms of the distribution of news in 'real time' and the capital-intensive advertising power that fuels this widespread dissemination. While continuing to operate under an older regime of civic, social and judicial protocols, newspapers are simultaneously threatened by political censorship.[24] Therefore, one may be able to access an image of dead bodies rotting on the banks of the Ganga on one's computer screen or on Instagram or Facebook, but one is not likely to see such an image on the front page of any Indian daily.

Note that I am focusing here on the Indian public sphere and media, which needs to be differentiated from its international counterparts, where images of the pandemic in the 'second wave' circulated widely, especially in publications like The New York Times, The Guardian, Der Spiegel, The Australian and others. At one level, this withholding of visual evidence of the pandemic in the Indian context is understandable because its manifestations were particularly harsh and immediate in our public domain. One could argue that conscientious editors of Indian newspapers chose not to show images of dead bodies on the banks of the Ganga—they could be considered too 'sensitive', far too 'disturbing' for public viewing.

---

24 From the 2022 World Press Freedom Index of Reporters Without Borders, we learn that India's position has slid from 142 to 150 out of 180 countries. Apart from new regulations of the digital media, the Indian government has also imposed tax raids, withdrawal of government advertising and charges of sedition on those media houses whose positions are perceived to be 'anti-national'. See Swaminathan S. Anklesaria Aiyar, 'How Rise of Low-Cost Guerrilla Media Aids Press Freedom', The Times of India, 15 May 2022: available at https://bit.ly/3yLvcLo

However, it could also be argued that such an erasure or omission needs to be linked to the widespread, yet tacit, censorship (and self-censorship) operating in Indian newspapers today, where an increasingly normalized work culture of fear prevails. For some time now, since the rise of Hindu majoritarianism, Indian editors have tended to play safe and couched their criticism in euphemisms and elisions of facts. More specifically, at a visual level, they have tended to downplay images that could be regarded as 'anti-national', or worse, 'anti-Hindu'. Admittedly, it remains possible to *write* about dead bodies in the Ganga, with allusions to earlier descriptions of such bodies made by veterans of Hindi literature like Suryakant Tripathy 'Nirala'. But most editors would not have the courage to accompany such write-ups with documentary photographic evidence.

Suryakant Tripathy, better known as Nirala, had witnessed death and suffering during the Spanish flu pandemic of 1918–19. In vivid prose, he had recalled, 'The Ganga is swollen with dead bodies.'[25] The anonymity of these bodies is juxtaposed with his forthright admission of personal loss:

> At my in-laws' house I learned that my wife had passed away. [...] My family disappeared in the blink of an eye. All our sharecroppers and labourers died, the four who worked for my cousin, as well as the two who worked for me. My cousin's eldest son was fifteen years old, my young daughter a year old. In whichever direction I turned, I saw darkness.[26]

---

25 Quoted in opening paragraph of Laura Spinney, 'Vital Statistics: How the Spanish Flu of 1918 Changed India', *The Caravan*, 19 October 2018: available at https://bityl.co/Auu0. See also Laura Spinney, *Pale Rider: The Spanish Flu of 1918 and How It Changed the World* (London: Vintage, 2018).
26 Spinney, 'Vital Statistics'.

Situating his personal losses within the larger global crisis of the Spanish flu pandemic, Nirala makes the small but significant point: 'The newspapers had informed us about the ravages of the epidemic.'[27]

In this regard, it is obligatory to point out that more than a century ago, between 1918 and 1919, it was the 'news' that mattered in newspapers, which were relatively divested of images and advertisements, not just in India but also in Britain, the United States and Europe. Today, in our increasingly image-driven media reportage, mirroring the 'society of the spectacle',[28] a report on the pandemic in India without images feels incomplete. At one level, this visual sobriety could be seen as a blessing in disguise, but one should not assume from this that the 'news' surrounding the pandemic is necessarily more substantial to make up for the loss of images.

Censorship, it could be argued, is not a new phenomenon in the history of pandemics. News of the initial outbreak of the Spanish flu in 1918 was actively censored by governments in the United States and Britain in order to avoid a demoralization of the Allied forces who were fighting the last months of the First World War. There are almost no photographs to be found of the early stages of that pandemic. Only by the end of the war, when censorship was no longer applicable or necessary, did photographs emerge in the public domain. A quick look at an assemblage of archetypal photographs, as reproduced in John M. Barry's *The Great Influenza* (2004),[29] albeit with a blatant American bias, reveals

---

27 Spinney, 'Vital Statistics'.

28 Guy Debord, *The Society of the Spectacle* (Donald Nicholson-Smith trans.) (New York: Zone Books, 1995).

29 John M. Barry, *The Great Influenza: The Story of the Deadliest Pandemic in History* (New York: Penguin, 2005).

very few images of dead bodies—for instance, of the casualties in Philadelphia, a city so grievously affected that the dead had to be interred in mass graves without coffins. In contrast, most of the images in the American archive radiate an aura of hygiene and medical supervision.

One could view these images as a study in white, because almost all of them are dominated by that colour—not just through the racial composition of the people documented in these images but also through the colour of the uniforms and masks worn by nurses and Red Cross volunteers, all dressed in immaculate white. There is also an omnipresence of white tents in makeshift shelters, and white linen on hundreds of beds in improvised hospitals, where the beds themselves are separated in some images by white screens. So, it is a relentlessly white world. Against this white, there is black—in the uniforms of the white-masked police and, above all, in the sheer proliferation of posters, black letters on white backgrounds, plastered on walls and the backs of tramcars: SPIT SPREADS DEATH! KEEP YOUR BEDROOM WINDOWS OPEN!

Needless to say, all these images read like 'good' government propaganda for the larger health and well-being of citizens. They are largely impersonal, if not official, and radiate a sense that the pandemic is under control by the government, the police and the medical services. At one level, this absence of intimacy in the images can be related to the overwhelming sense of fatigue and ennui felt by a people who had endured the war for four years. By the time the war ended in November 1918, this sense of exhaustion had deepened as people continued to die, in even larger numbers than during the war, on account of this mysterious killer influenza. So little was known about this influenza at a medical level and even less about how it needed to be treated. For the longest time it was linked to a bacterium called 'Pfeiffer's baccilus' rather than a virus. There were no antibiotics, ventilators or sustained oxygen treatment available. Almost as a compensation, governments and civic services went out of their way to demonstrate their 'care' for citizens through information campaigns relating to protection and large-scale disinfection projects. In this official reportage of dealing with the pandemic, there is a relative dearth, if not total absence, of 'personal', i.e. non-official, photographs.

The situation in India is even more bleak across all sectors of society. Historian David Arnold, who has studied the Spanish flu pandemic in the Indian context with considerable rigor, building on his earlier research on the plague in Bombay from 1896 onwards, among other diseases, has pointed out to me in correspondence: 'There are no visuals of the [Spanish flu] epidemic [in India] that I know of any kind whatsoever. It's always US images that are used for India, which is iconographic nonsense.'[30] Arnold goes on to acknowledge that this absence of images cannot be related to any 'active censorship' or to the dearth of camera film, even as these factors may not be entirely ruled out in order to account for the pictorial void that one associates with the pandemic in India.

In contrast, according to Arnold, there is considerable visual evidence of the 1896 plague in Bombay, including images of cremation pyres, although not in the large numbers that we have

---

30 David Arnold's authoritative study *Colonizing the Body: State Medicine and Epidemic Disease in Nineteenth Century India* (Berkeley and Los Angeles: University of California Press, 1993) covers smallpox, cholera and the plague. On the Spanish flu pandemic (or 'epidemic' as he prefers to name it), Arnold has written 'Death and the Modern Empire: The 1918–19 Influenza Epidemic in India', *Transactions of the Royal Historical Society* 29 (2019): 181–200. On the more recent pandemic, he has published 'Pandemic India: Coronavirus and the Uses of History', *Journal of Asian Studies* 79(3) (August 2020): 569–77. I am grateful to David Arnold for sharing his views with me on photography in the pandemic on 23 June 2021.

today of cremations during the pandemic in 2020–21. Likewise, while there are many more images of hospitals with decaying infrastructures in India today, the significant difference with the plague years in Bombay is that those hospitals were presented as iconic structures of imperialist vigilance. The colonial state's aura of concern for its subjects needs to be juxtaposed with the violent opposition of large sections of the Indian population to the brutally insensitive invasion of individual homes by the colonial administration through its coercive drives of mass disinfection and civic hygiene. As Arnold has substantiated in considerable detail, this overt medicalization of the body violated caste taboos and community protocols relating to touch and human interaction. The hospitalization of Indian women in particular challenged norms of gender and traditional boundaries between the 'private' and 'public' domains of life.

Against this larger historical context, Arnold makes his point succinctly: 'Between 1896–98, when the image of the hospital was shown, it was one of intended calm and magisterial order in the face of the overwhelming panic and chaos outside. Now, panic and chaos have come to epitomize the hospital itself.'[31]

OWNERSHIP

It would be useful here to inscribe, however briefly, the role played by corporate and media houses in the ownership and dissemination of images in the digital media. It is chastening to be reminded that almost all the images of the pandemic that we have been able to access are available on the websites of some of the largest media agencies of the world, notably Getty Images, Reuters, BBC and CNN. These corporations *own* the images, if not physically then

---

31 Correspondence with author, 23 June 2021.

through the rights of global distribution, and in this crucial sense they control the visibility of the pandemic in the world at large.[32]

Significantly, at the level of production, all the photographs of the pandemic in India have been shot by predominantly Indian photographers *in situ*, in the harshest and most localized of circumstances. While the photographers are named, the role of 'fixers' in setting up the locations and hiring special equipment (like 'drones' for aerial shots), remains largely undocumented. The process of shooting these photographs was rough, so much so that it is unlikely that formal permissions to record cremations and the final moments of dying patients were possible. In these circumstances, where almost everything was left to chance and accident, it is, indeed, ironic that these photographs of local tragedies have landed up being 'protected' in the most capital-intensive of global archives. For all the alleged 'democratization' of images in global media archives and social-media networks, one needs to keep in mind that these images are highly patented and come with a price.

Today, corporate and media houses control the distribution of images. Earlier, national governments controlled images relating to war, famine or disease. Significantly, photographers today do not necessarily have to be officially affiliated to a news agency or television station for their photographs to be represented on global websites. Unlike, for instance, Siddiqui and Abidi, who were part of the Reuters photography team, the independent photographer Shukla was also in a position to sell his images of the dead bodies in the Ganga on the Getty website, where he is identified as a

---

32 In 2016 Getty earned the rights to distribute 100 million photos and 800,000 videos of Corbis Images, previously owned by Bill Gates, who sold his collection to the new media company Visual China Group. See Michael Zhang, 'Corbis Images Sold by Bill Gates to Visual China Group', *PetaPixel*, 22 January 2016: available at https://https://bityl.co/BdEL

'stringer'. The language accompanying the hard-sell of his 'premium high-res photos' is downright crass. Inevitably, when one encounters such blatant commercialism in selling images of dead bodies, it is hard to avoid falling back on a nationalist-nativist reflex that condemns the selling of 'Third World misery' to the world at large. One is compelled to acknowledge that the overwhelming majority of these images have called attention to the extreme and occasionally exotic representation of the spectacle of death and suffering. In these images, funerals and moments of private grief have been relentlessly opened to a voyeuristic global gaze. Almost inevitably, such a phenomenon runs the risk of playing into nationalist outrage: *How dare they represent us in this way?*

In contrast to this visceral reflex, a more critical response would be that while global capitalism devours images, it also facilitates their distribution at a phenomenal level, circumventing all possible attempts to censor the suffering of millions of people during the pandemic. We can—indeed, we must—question how the pandemic can become a spectacle in this onslaught of photographs, made possible by the most sophisticated of cameras and drones. However, we cannot deny that these images, many of them too searing in their impact to be witnessed in a dispassionate mode, represent real events. One may question their modes of representation and capitulations to sensationalism and voyeurism, but, at a purely empirical level, the two men lying in a hospital bed, the man running through a cremation ground, and even the most extreme image of dead bodies on the banks of the Ganga were not fictions. In this sense, they have a political value—they show us what the Indian state would prefer us not to see in its concerted attempt to manufacture amnesia in a state of undeclared emergency.

I insert this brief note on the corporate ownership of the visuality of the pandemic to acknowledge that we are dealing with a contradictory phenomenon. On the one hand, what we are made to see on our computers and smartphones runs the risk of playing into a consumerism of misery. On the other hand, the sheer intimacy and proximity with which we are exposed to the harshest manifestations of human suffering and social injustice inadvertently offer a resistance to the attempted censorship and whitewashing of images at national levels. If global corporations cannot be credited with either altruism or compassion in their distribution of the images, neither can national governments be credited for an ethics of care in dealing with the sentiments and feelings of their citizens. Both phenomena are manifestations of a colossal indifference to human suffering and, in this regard, one could argue that even as they may seem to be virulently opposed to each other at an ideological level, they are symbiotically linked at subterranean levels in their promotion of capital and power.

THE LONG WALK

Let us turn now to a different set of images and to a more experiential engagement with the pandemic. Here the focus of my reflections will be on the *affect* of photography and its sensitization to the struggle of people in surviving the pandemic. If the 'second wave' of the ongoing pandemic in India is marked by images of disease and death, focusing on hospitals, cremation grounds and dead bodies, the 'first phase' between March and September 2020 will be remembered for images of an almost impossible resilience as millions of people, primarily labourers and city-based contract workers, walked back to their village homes once the national lockdown was imposed. The photographs of this period testify to the desperation of people wanting to return home at all costs, which necessitated crossing state borders and walking hundreds of miles; the photographs also affirm how people fell back on their own resources when the State failed to protect their most basic rights. To speak of the violation of rights is almost euphemistic because, in essence, people had no rights that one would expect of citizens following the lockdown.

In actuality, the vast mass of people whom we see in these images are 'citizens' at a nominal level, even as they may not be not fully established members of 'civil society'. Rather, in the terminology of Partha Chatterjee, they can be more readily identified as belonging to 'political society', whose inhabitants live precariously in the marginalized hinterlands of cities, where they provide the labour to keep the infrastructures and services of the city alive.[33] Denied the basic necessities of life, and surviving from hand to mouth, these survivors have been identified in the vast literature surrounding the pandemic as 'migrants'. More precisely, they are 'internal migrants' insofar as they cross borders within the framework of the nation-state, and in this sense, they need to be differentiated from those migrants seeking shelter, employment and citizenship in Europe as they flee different states of oppression back home. Neither are these 'internal migrants' to be associated with 'foreign labour', as in the large constituencies of workers from India and Bangladesh who constitute the vast majority of construction workers in countries like Singapore. Their migration is based on strictly contractual terms with explicit rules and regulations.

I spell out these distinctions to emphasize the cruel but basic fact that the 'internal migrants' who surfaced during the first lockdown in India are *our own people*. They are not from elsewhere— they are *not* refugees. However, one could argue that the brutal conditions which compelled them to flee the cities during the

---

33 Partha Chatterjee, *Lineages of Political Society: Studies in Postcolonial Democracy* (New York: Columbia University Press, 2011).

lockdown and return to their rural homes have transformed them into some other entity. I am tempted to describe their condition as *becoming a refugee in one's own country*, divested of fundamental rights and basic securities.

Against this background, it would be useful to situate the representation of 'internal refugees' with other photographic *oeuvres* that it may seem to resemble. Let us focus for the moment on the phenomenon of crowds. The Indian photographic *oeuvre* has been massively represented by vast crowds of people, as in the swirling masses of pilgrims to be found in the Kumbh Mela and other pilgrim sites like Sabarimala, Amarnath, Vaishno Devi, Manasarovar, some of them involving their own versions of 'long walks' from one sacred site to another.[34] Photographer and cultural critic Sadanand Menon has pointed out how the 'long-walk pilgrimage traditions', particularly of the Varkari *sampradaya* of pilgrims walking to Pandharpur in Maharashtra to receive the darshan of the god Vitthala, following the tradition set up by Bhakti poets like Namdeo and Tukaram, offers a stark contrast to the 'blank, denuded-of-hope walk of the migrant labourers returning home post-lockdown'.[35] Indeed, one must emphasize there is no sense of a pilgrimage in the 'long walk' of labourers. Rather, it is the desperate reverse journey of people fleeing the city to remain alive; the shrine, if any, is 'home', which is less a place of belonging than an emergency shelter.

---

34 Sadanand Menon, correspondence with author, 22 December 2021.

35 Menon, correspondence with author. I am grateful to Menon for calling to my attention Rajula Shah's documentary on the long-walk pilgrimage tradition in her documentary film *Chalo Sakha Us Des Mein* (At Home Walking). This documentary provides the basis for his astute reflection on the different kinds of walks that characterize pilgrimages in contrast to the flight of internal migrant labourers to their rural homes.

Neither can the photographic *oeuvre* of Indian labourers compare with other visual archives from the 1970s of migrant labourers from Italy and Turkey seeking temporary employment in Germany, among other developed capitalist societies. In this context, John Berger's precise political observations on the plight of such migrants in A *Seventh Man*, accompanying Jean Mohr's searing photographs and portraits of migrant labourers, are built on the fact that, 'In Germany (and in Britain) one out of seven manual workers is an immigrant.'[36] Much has changed over the years since the publication of Berger's book in 1975, not least the more recent brutality of migrants fleeing African countries to Europe in overcrowded boats, many of which capsized, resulting in thousands of them drowning. The Berger/Mohr photographic documentation does not show the dead bodies of migrants, not least because the scenario of migration being recorded in the 1970s would appear to be a lot more 'civilized'. But, underlying this civility, or, reinforcing this masquerade of civility, one encounters different states of dehumanization and humiliation. Thus, in Mohr's black-and-white photographs, we see the migrants stripped naked as they are subjected to medical examinations; we see them lying on bunks in cramped quarters with vacant expressions; we see them attempting to survive the degradation and terror of skinning animals in abattoirs. In this dehumanized state, the migrants also have moments of celebration, punctuated by acts of cooking, eating, drinking and smoking, always driven by the need to survive and earn as much money for the family back home. For me, the most poignant, yet stark evidence of the migrant's strategy of survival is to be found in a photograph of a migrant's face, one half of which is torn before he leaves home

---

36 John Berger and Jean Mohr, *A Seventh Man: The Story of a Migrant Worker in Europe* (Cambridge: Granta Books, 1989 [1975]).

while the other half is returned to the family after he has crossed the border, whereupon the full amount of money has to be paid by the family to the agent for the safe passage.[37]

I turn to A *Seventh Man* to offer a radically different point of reference for the 'internal migration' of Indian labourers during the lockdown. For a start, the migration of Turkish and Italian labourers to Europe is a *choice* that has been made out of the harsh realization that there is no money to be made in the villages for at least six months in the year. This is not substantially different from the predicament of Indian labourers who migrate on a seasonal or long-term duration to support families back home, even as there are increasingly more employment opportunities in rural areas for labourers not to migrate long distances to the cities. The photographs of Indian labourers post-lockdown is also driven by choice, but it is a *desperate* choice—a life-and-death choice—that is based less on earning a living than on the necessity of fleeing the city in order to survive. Home, in this predicament, is not so much a destination or a repository of rest and comfort—it is more like the only place where one can hope to exist.

Another stark difference is to be found in the omnipresence of male migrant workers in the Berger/Mohr collection of photographs. This contrasts sharply with the photographs of Indian male labourers, who are seen, more often than not, with their families, notably wives and children, carrying an assemblage of their household belongings like buckets and trunks and bundles of clothes. It is not just solitary and alienated labourers who are on the road, but also entire communities. Countering an earlier populist slogan that 'the nation is on the move', we see here another *movement*—of the most marginalized sectors of Indian society

---

37 Berger and Mohr, *A Seventh Man*, p. 45.

turning away en masse from their abandoned sites of employment to the poverty back home.

PROBLEMATIZING DURATION

The archive of images around labourers returning home could be the subject of a book in its own right, such is the scale and power of the images. For my purpose here, I would like to build an argument around a provocation put forward by philosopher Soumyabrata Choudhury which works against the grain of sentimental humanism to which images of the destitute are particularly prone:

> We must caution ourselves against receiving the possible and real migrant walk today as an *image*. I do not deny those unbearable images of entire families walking under a remorseless summer sky. Yet I propose that the real of these impossible journeys is not accessible either to the pathos of an image or to the tragic pleasure of a narrative. Today writers, dramatists and filmmakers might weave tender and cathartic 'stories' from this unbearable history. But they will still not have served their art well unless they grasp the real *duration* of these impossible migrations.[38]

In this cogently formulated position, Choudhury inscribes his own ambivalence between rejecting the reduction of the pain and suffering of migrants to an 'image', even as he does not deny the power of 'those unbearable images'. While one can assume that Choudhury has seen these images, he does not directly describe any of them. In an anti-representational mode of analysis,

---

[38] Soumyabrata Choudhury, *Now It's Come to Distances: Notes on Shaheen Bagh and Coronavirus, Association and Isolation* (New Delhi: Navayana, 2020), pp. 167–8.

he denies any easy translation of the migrants' 'impossible journeys' into the accessible 'pathos' of an image or the 'tragic pleasure' of a narrative. Without quite spelling it out, Choudhury seems to be sceptical of the cathartic implications of such images and narratives. Nonetheless, he continues to believe that artists from different disciplines 'might weave' new narratives from this 'unbearable history'. But this would only be possible if artists could recognize 'the real *duration*' of these 'impossible' migrations.

Significantly, the ethical dilemma of representing migration seems to focus in the final analysis on grasping the role of 'duration' in multiple journeys. While Choudhury seems to be speaking of the arts in general, I would like to sharpen the focus by problematizing 'duration' in the context of photography, not least because it is in photographs that the migrants' journeys have been most prodigiously recorded. Theatre productions and fictions have yet to emerge in response to this ordeal: it is going to take time before anything like 'tragic pleasure' is likely to be available while watching a play on the migrants, assuming that such plays will be written. In this context, it is worth recalling how one of the worst catastrophes and man-made tragedies in India, the Bengal Famine of 1943–44, was represented in the landmark Bengali theatre production of Bijon Bhattacharya's *Nabanna* (The New Harvest), even as people starving to death on the streets of Calcutta continued to remain a harsh reality.[39]

---

39 *Nabanna* was an iconic production of the Indian Peoples' Theatre Association (IPTA), a landmark in the exploration of epic realism in the Indian theatrical context. The translation of Bijon Bhattacharya's play text along with an introduction can be read in Arjun Ghosh's *Nabanna, Of Famine and Resilience: A Play* (New Delhi: Rupa, 2019). Amartya Sen's *Poverty and Famines: An Essay on Entitlement and Deprivation* (Oxford: Clarendon Press, 1981) remains the definitive economic study of the Bengal Famine in the larger context of its 'man-made' causes and strategies by the colonial government.

Against this stirring example of representing a state of emergency in all its immediacy and complexity, my sense is that the pandemic that we are experiencing today is not likely to be envisioned either theatrically or cinematically for quite some time.

Returning to photography, which remains the most viable and accessible domain for visualizing the pandemic, we need to problematize whether its representation can deal with the dynamics of 'duration'. All readings of 'duration' in photography, I would argue, need to begin with an understanding of the 'instant'. In photography, we are made aware of how the incandescent instant of recording an image is embedded in the split-second connection between the person / thing / event being photographed and the mind's eye of the photographer. This instant is almost always an interstice between a 'before' and an 'after'—what happened before a particular photograph was taken, and what happened immediately after. At times, there is a strong temporal sense that the action or gesture caught in the photograph will continue to be made after the photograph has been shot; at other times, there is no guarantee that the same action or gesture will be repeated.

No one has been able to capture the phenomenology of this instant more precisely, yet evocatively, than Barthes in his homage to chemists who first called attention to the 'luminous rays emitted by a variously lighted object', which, in essence, makes any photograph an 'emanation' of the referent.

> From a real body, which was there, proceed radiations which ultimately touch me, who am here; the duration of the transmission is insignificant; the photograph of the missing being, as Sontag says, will touch me like the delayed rays of a star. A sort of umbilical cord links the body of the photographed thing to my gaze: light, though

impalpable, is here a carnal medium, a skin I share with anyone who has been photographed.[40]

It could be argued that this physics-driven 'emanation' of the photograph emerging from 'real' bodies has little to do with the 'real duration' of journeys made by migrants. Indeed, in a passing remark in the passage quoted above, Barthes emphasizes that the 'duration' of the transmission of light from object through the photograph to the body of the person perceiving the image is 'insignificant'. What ultimately matters for him is that the transmission of light registers in the viewer's body at a tactile level in a momentary communion.

Pushing the point further, it could be argued that the instantaneous capturing of the 'real' in any photograph almost inevitably results in a fragmentation of reality, where the absence of a *sequence* of events renders the sense of 'duration' almost impossible. What we see in any image is what exists—or, more precisely, existed— at a particular moment. Arguably, while this may be the case for how the ontology of photography has been canonized, one of the most robust developments in the photography of the 'second wave' has been the decision made by some press photographers to present their images through assemblages or longer narratives. Here we are presented with a multitude of 'instants' of reality. It is through these new forms of structuring images in sequence that we sense the *duration* of 'impossible journeys', as the photographer follows not one family but several families who are all part of a larger state of emergency, moving from one point to the next, in what would seem like a limitless stretch of time.

One of the strongest examples of this *oeuvre* of 'durational photography' is to be found in the video footage of photographs compiled by Bandeep Singh, Group Photo Editor, *India Today*, who

---

40 Barthes, *Camera Lucida*, p. 80.

has documented, with a strong sense of engagement and empathy, the labourers returning to their homes.[41] Supplementing the video is a commentary which calls attention to the significant details in the photographs. Admittedly, this is not a contrapuntal narrative on the lines advocated by Sekula, where 'film and video, sound and image, or sound, image, and text can be worked *over* and *against* each other, leading to the possibility of negation and metacommentary'.[42] Singh's reportage is far less complicated in its intention—voice, image, photograph and video work in sync rather than in disjunction to create a dynamic visual narrative, extending over an entire day, from morning to night. During this time, we see hundreds of migrants walking on highways, occasionally catching their breath, and, at times, sleeping in a state of exhaustion.

From the opening beats of the narrative, one is struck by the cumulative speed of the journey. I will quote at length from Singh's commentary:

> My first impression is how fast they walk—frictionless, pulled towards the direction of their home, towards a sliver of hope, towards even a rumour [...] that there will be a bus. Kids walk faster, to keep pace with their parents. Mothers, with kids on waists, sacks on their heads, walking with their mouths covered by their saree pallus. I notice they don't fall back in the group. None is out of breath. Families walk in groups, formed by their destinations. There is no leader, no instructions. Yet they stop, rest and then get up to walk all at once, wordlessly, like the synchronic movement of a shoal of fish.[43]

---

41 Bandeep Singh, '90 Km with Migrant Hope: Capturing Exodus of Migrant Workers in 13 Stills', *India Today*, 15 April 2020: available at https:/bityl.co/ Auuq
42 Sekula, 'Dismantling Modernism, Reinventing Documentary', p. 869.
43 Singh, '90 Km with Migrant Hope'.

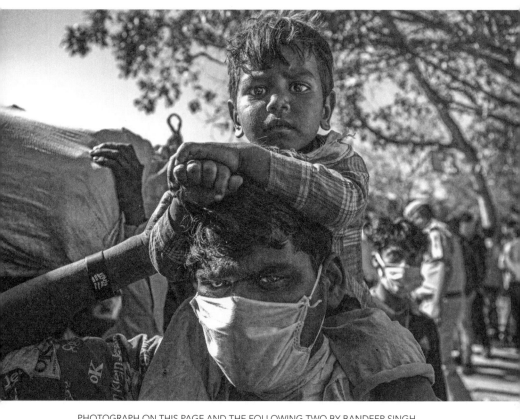

PHOTOGRAPH ON THIS PAGE AND THE FOLLOWING TWO BY BANDEEP SINGH

This relentless walk continues from morning to night, occasionally breaking into a run as the workers and their families rush towards a bus that is already too full. At times a photographer is mistaken for a policeman, causing the workers to 'disperse like startled pigeons' and jump over railings to get off the main road. At times they are walking in the wrong direction, involuntarily extending the duration of their journey. 'Kahan ja rahe ho?' [Where are you going?], Singh asks a group of migrants to learn that they are heading towards Gorakhpur, Uttar Pradesh, for which they need to catch a bus from Pari Chowk in Greater Noida. Before he can provide directions, the migrants have already moved far ahead. He recalls shouting after them, 'But Pari Chowk is down the road on the opposite side, the flyover will take [you] to the wrong side and [you] won't get to know until [you] reach the police barrier almost 2 kilometres away!' But the migrants have moved on, and Singh's attempt to help shorten their journey is in vain. It is through such time lags and moments of getting lost that one is able to sense the extended duration of the journeys that the migrants seem to accept with stoic determination.

There are many other details in Singh's journey with the migrants that I cannot elaborate on here. Suffice it to say that they are deeply sensitive to the interstices of time, movement and light, so much so that he can make us see a child tucked around the waist of his mother leaning out and playing with his shadow bouncing on the road. At times Singh captures not the walk but the agony of waiting for a lift, the father holding out his hand for a vehicle to pass, the mother in the background grimacing out of sheer exhaustion, the young daughter looking defiant with her hands around her waist. More poignantly, Singh makes us see in a group of five a young man with polio 'hobbling his way wearing a purple shirt and a fluorescent smile.' He asks them:

'How far do you aim to go like this?'

'Till Agra.'

'*Par kyun?*' [But why?]

'*Yahan kya karenge. Sab paise bhi khatam ho gaya hain.*' [What to do here. All our money is finished.]

I follow them for five minutes and want to help. '*Yeh rakh lo, raste me kaam aayega*' [Here, keep this. It will be useful on the road.]—I offer them a Rs. 500 note.

They all stop, slowly surround me, two of them with folded hands. '*Iski zaroorat nai hai, please yeh mat deejiye. Aapne pooch liya yahi kaafi hai.*' [There is no need for this, please don't give us this. The fact that you have asked is enough.][44]

It is through such conversations that the duration of any journey, however onerous, can be humanized and enlivened, but also stretched. I have deliberately slowed down my narrative to make space for such conversations in order to make the point that photographs accompanied by reportage can succeed in creating a sense of duration that may not be readily experienced when we see photographs in their atomized state—each image enclosed in itself, radiating a particular moment in life. In Singh's reportage, we experience more than one life and more than one sense of time, in a cumulative experience of migration that is at once affecting and thought-provoking.

---

44 Singh, '90 Km with Migrant Hope'. The unexpected civility in this exchange, where money is not the issue but the sheer concern of one human being for another, is reminiscent of many such encounters narrated in Mander, *Locking Down the Poor*.

REPRESENTING JAMLO

On a more realistic note, it would be inaccurate to say that all journeys of migrants get reported with empathy and warmth. Some journeys are not reported at all, and it is their duration which remains most opaque, if not unknown. I am thinking here of the journey of the 12-year-old Adivasi (tribal) girl Jamlo Madkam, who walked 140 km from a chilli farm in Telangana where she was working as a labourer to her home in Aded in the Bijapur district of Chhattisgarh. Shortly before reaching her destination—some reports indicate that it was as little as 11 km; others indicate a distance of 55–60 km—she collapsed and died of electrolyte imbalance and exhaustion.[45]

Such a tragedy is hard to address in words. Nor would there seem to be any photograph that we can hold on to of Jamlo beyond her identification in her Aadhar card. Her death would appear too painful, too harsh to be 'represented' in any available narrative, at least for the moment. However, it would be sad, and even disturbing, if we accepted that Jamlo and her condition, shared by many of her rural compatriots, cannot be represented. In this regard, it is quite astonishing that the only 'fictional' representation of Jamlo's life to date happens to be a children's illustrated picture book titled *Jamlo Walks*.[46] The sheer courage of this endeavour, by documentary filmmaker, writer and teacher Samina Mishra,

---

45 Purusottam Thakur and Kamlesh Painkra, 'Jamlo's Last Journey along a Locked-Down Road', *People's Archive of Rural India* (PARI), 14 May 2020: available at https://bityl.co/BavX; Gargi Verma, '12-Year-Old Walks 100 Km, Dies Just Short of Bijapur Home', *The Indian Express*, 21 April 2020: available at https://bityl.co/Av1m.

46 *Jamlo Walks: An Illustrated Book about Life During Lockdown* (New Delhi: Puffin Books, 2021) is written by documentary filmmaker and teacher Samina Mishra with illustrations by Tarique Aziz. I am grateful to Jerry Pinto for calling my attention to this book.

needs to be duly acknowledged, given the risks of appropriating Jamlo's life for the purpose of a children's book with a predominantly urban middle-class readership in English: a world far removed from the realities of child labour where the basic right to education is summarily denied, even as it exists in law.

Mishra is well aware of these risks even as she resolves not to 'reduce' Jamlo only to 'the girl who died walking'. This premise is sensitively expressed in Tarique Aziz's bold and striking visuals that illustrate the story—he opts for a bright spectrum of colours, notably a 'blue sky', which was one of the manifestations of the lockdown across India, when pollution levels decreased and nature seemed to be rejuvenated even as people were dying in large numbers. Hence, the almost surreal quality of hundreds of flamingos nesting in a creek in the urban sprawl of Navi Mumbai, and the heavenly sight of the snow-peaked Himalayas magically visible again after many years from the industrial town of Saharanpur, Uttar Pradesh. The lockdown opened glimmers, and occasionally vistas of the imagination that almost made one wonder how human tragedy could coexist with the startling beauty of nature and the re-animation of the bird and animal worlds.

This observation compels us to question how the imagination is mobilized in the telling of *Jamlo Walks*. Does it have a vibrant energy of its own, or is it there to illustrate the story in an instrumentalist manner? As much as Mishra does not want to reduce Jamlo to 'the girl who died walking', the reality is that Jamlo walked an enormous distance that resulted in her death. The title of Mishra's book itself seizes the key word 'Jamlo *Walks*'. The most vibrant sections of the narrative focus on Jamlo *walking*, past fields, on empty streets, with a bag of chillis slung on her shoulders— her wages for her work on the chilli fields until the lockdown. Against this harsh economic reality, there is at least one wondrous moment when Jamlo, hungry and exhausted, offers a dry chilli to a bird who flies away.

Against the subtle dynamics of this moment, Jamlo's walk is truncated by insertions of stories relating to three other children from middle-class backgrounds, one of whom watches her mother surfing the Internet on her laptop to watch the labourers returning home; another sees the *jhuggi* (slum) cluster near his house being sealed off by civic authorities; and yet another takes a glass of cold water from the fridge during his online class. None of these children are in any way linked to Jamlo—they are there to make the reader aware of the obvious social disparities between Jamlo's world and the more privileged one of educated, urban children.

I am not sure whether such juxtapositions 'work' apart from highlighting the didactic nature of the narrative where something needs to be 'told' to the young middle-class readers of *Jamlo Walks*. Didacticism, as writer Jerry Pinto and theatre artist and teacher Maya Krishna Rao have shared with me, is one of the dominant tendencies in contemporary children's literature, where it seems almost obligatory that children have to be given a moral in order to better 'understand' the story. This goes totally against the grain of earlier traditions of children's literature in the Indian context where there were more flights of fantasy and freedom of imagination and no accompanying moral to the story.[47]

And yet, one could argue, how far can imagination go when one is trying to tell a 'real story', however positively, about a young girl who died in cruel and unjust circumstances? Here, Mishra settles for a safe choice by making Jamlo fall asleep while imagining a return home to her parents. Her 'death' is suggested by a two-page

---

47 This point is made with considerable force by folklorist and oral historian Komal Kothari in my book *Rajasthan: An Oral History; Conversations with Komal Kothari* (New Delhi: Penguin, 2003), pp. 19–20.

visual in which a pair of torn chappals and a leaf resting on it are juxtaposed with the distant figures of a father and mother. This opens up yet another troubling trope in the politics of children's literature: Can children not deal with death? Fairy tales and nursery rhymes, as we know, have never been free of violence and death. And yet, increasingly, there is a need for political correctness from some educators that censors any possibility of pain on the grounds that children may not be able to cope with the harsh realities of life. Are we to assume that the children reading a copy of *Jamlo Walks* would not know that she has died?

I realize that there are no easy solutions here and that there are different narrative strategies that need to be contextualized within different cultures. In the burgeoning market of children's books in the West, for instance, which have been designed for adults to share with young readers, there are any number of stories and illustrated informational texts where death and bereavement are communicated with gentle and creative inflections.[48] And yet, while acknowledging the reassuring power of these stories in addressing the reality of death as a fact of life in the natural world, which has the potential to enable a child to accept the death of a grandparent or a pet dog, I would have to acknowledge that Jamlo's death presents a much harsher social context. Even as I respect Mishra's sincerity in not wanting to appropriate or sensationalize it, I get the sense that Jamlo's last walk has not been fully imagined. While the author's sincerity is substantiated in an appendix by a

---

48 See, for instance, Holly Webb's 'Top 10 Children's Books on Death and Bereavement', *The Guardian*, 5 February 2015: available at: https://bityl.co/ Bavc. Also, Jillian Roberts, *What Happens When a Loved One Dies? Our First Talk About Death* (Cindy Revell illus.), 'Just Enough' Series No. 2 (Victoria, Canada: Orca Book Publishers, 2016). I am grateful to Becky Britton Pillai for calling my attention to these books.

somewhat academic note titled 'The Covid-19 Pandemic', one wishes that she could have found a way of incorporating the realities of the lockdown *within* Jamlo's imaginary as child. What exists at the moment is a sense of well-meaning adults trying to teach children about the cruelties of life, which in some way infantilizes the capacity of children to recognize what is going on around them.

In a different format from fiction, one can learn about Jamlo from her inscription in the epic documentation of migrant workers and labourers to be found on the website of PARI (People's Archive of Rural India), which was one of the sources for *Jamlo Walks*.[49] PARI's founder editor P. Sainath has set a standard for his robust reportage of rural poverty over decades of engaged journalism and photography. It would be useful to know how PARI would be in a position to reach out to child labourers from Jamlo's community in their own language. There is no one way of intervening through Jamlo's story; there are many possibilities and forums of interaction. One can only hope that Jamlo's last 'journey' as represented in the PARI website will inspire narratives and films that wait to be made in her memory and struggle. Whether or not they will elicit 'tragic pleasure', to invoke one of the categories raised by Choudhury earlier in this section, is less important to my mind than finding ways in which Jamlo's life is duly recognized and honoured.

---

49 The PARI website, a multimedia digital journalism platform, is accessible at https://ruralindiaonline.org/en/

ETHICS OF CRYING

Shifting ethical considerations into a more emotional and personal register, I would acknowledge that the photographs of the pandemic which struck me most deeply were those *not* made by the most accomplished professionals in the field. This is a somewhat odd acknowledgement, given my deep appreciation of the powerfully constructed images by stalwarts like Siddiqui and Abidi. But, to be honest, I was more emotionally affected by those images taken by relatively unknown photographers who chose to focus not on the epic scale of the tragedy but on very ordinary— one could say, banal—images of family members crying and holding on to each other, following the death of a loved one. I am not trying to make an argument here that the 'amateur' images were more 'authentic' than the 'professional' ones; I am merely attempting to account for what moved me at a personal level.

As I found myself surfing hundreds of images on my laptop in an almost voyeur-like state, occasionally numbed into silent witnessing, it was these direct exposures to people crying and clinging to each other, without the surreal camouflage of personal protective equipment and gowns, that both made me cry and think of the ethics of crying during a pandemic: crying that is involuntary, sudden, which takes one by surprise and leaves one choked. Facing such a visceral rupture in one's state of being, which may last for only a few seconds but leaves one shaken, it becomes particularly odious to be reminded of the Solicitor General of India's derisive words, 'Let's try and not be a cry baby.'[50]

---

50 This statement is included in Roy, 'We Are Witnessing a Crime against Humanity'. On 24 April 2021, on the very day when more deaths occurred resulting from the shortage of oxygen at Jaipur Golden Hospital, Solicitor General Tushar Mehta, representing the government of India in the Delhi High Court, said: 'Let's try and not be a cry baby [. . .] so far we have ensured that no one in the country was left without oxygen.'

These words were uttered with contempt in response to the Delhi government's plea for increased oxygen allocation.

With her consummate ability to pierce through the political deceptions of any crisis, Arundhati Roy uses these insidious words as a leitmotif that splices the facts in her chillingly accurate report on India's Covid catastrophe titled 'We Are Witnessing a Crime against Humanity'. In a freewheeling yet meticulously structured article that covers the controversy over the Kumbh Mela pilgrimage which became a 'superspreader' event,[51] along with the elections in West Bengal where Prime Minister Modi and Home Minister Amit Shah actively canvassed for votes 'like vultures' in mass election rallies even as the virus was spreading, Roy inserts the insidious words with devastating irony: 'Let's try and not be a cry baby.' Only now the context has changed from the non-availability of oxygen to the mendacity of the ruling party determined to go ahead with its political agenda at all costs, regardless of its impact on the lives of people. Roy's rhetorical device is not just reminiscent of fierce satire, but also a reminder of the stonewalling facade of the government, which refuses to show any remorse for its gross mismanagement of the pandemic, still less any acknowledgement of its absence of responsibility.

Returning to the ethics of crying in response to the grief of unknown families, I would emphasize that this is not a question of *Regarding the Pain of Others* (2003), as Susan Sontag has formulated in a partial rewrite of her earlier classic *On Photography*

---

51 For an incisive analysis of how the Kumbh Mela, one of the largest pilgrimage gatherings held in India, was supported by the Government of India in collusion with the Hindu religious organization of the Akhil Bharatiya Akhada Parishad, read Shuddhabrata Sengupta, 'Kumbh 2021: Astrology, Mortality, and the Indifference to Life of Leaders and Stars', *The Wire*, 20 April 2021: available at https://bityl.co/Bavs

(1977).[52] In the later book, which is largely about the devastating impact of war, she is less critical of the appropriative and aggressive dimensions of photography and more open to its empathetic possibilities and long-term implications beyond the camera's first encounter of a scene of suffering. When I see an Indian family crying for a loved one they have lost to the virus, they are not 'others' for me. And I am not 'regarding' them. I am affected as much for myself and whatever surrounds me in the ruins of what I am compelled to call 'my country' with an immediacy of feeling that cuts through me rather like a 'wound'. Perhaps, this is analogous, though not identical, to how Barthes has theorized at least one of the many manifestations of the punctum, which exists not just as a 'detail' but also as an undying memory.

To what extent will photographs of the pandemic be remembered in the inner recesses of memory? This is an open question. It is more than likely that the 'public' images of the pandemic, as embodied in the images of Siddiqui, Abidi and Shukla, will be forgotten, or relegated to the archives. In contrast, the more intimate photographs taken by family members of their loved ones will be cherished and preserved in wallets and albums. Needless to say, these photographs are likely to be pre-pandemic reminders of how people looked before they took ill and were rushed to the hospital or died at home, untouched and treated like sources of contagion. In this regard, we need to remind ourselves that the moment of death during the pandemic for thousands of casualties has remained largely unrecorded. People died alone. In most cases, family members had no access to the bodies of their loved ones, which were dumped in body bags and cremated anonymously. While we have many images of body bags and coffins across the world, we have almost no images of the dead themselves.

---

52 Susan Sontag, *Regarding the Pain of Others* (New York: Farrar, Straus and Giroux, 2003).

As a global phenomenon, the pandemic has almost flaunted its invisibility. For all the lurid multicoloured, surreal sketches bordering on kitsch that have been made of the coronavirus—with a crown and spiky protuberances on its spherical body—the virus itself remains invisible. Its symptoms have continued to be so deceptively mild that most people seem to have come to terms with the coronavirus as an 'ordinary' flu. Unlike other viruses, there are no external manifestations—no rashes, no lesions, no scars. Most enigmatically, and dangerously, this virus can exist in asymptomatic conditions, so that one could be a carrier without being aware of it. The talismanic power of the vaccine, with its double dose and booster shots, lulls us into thinking that the situation is controllable. But such is the volatility underlying this seeming control that there can be a precipitous turn for the worse the moment a persistent fever or a breathing problem gets out of control, or 'co-morbidities' complicate the recovery process.

Invisibility deepens from this stage onwards, as the patient is double-masked, shrouded in protective gear and rushed to a hospital where he or she is isolated with no contact with the outside world apart from the medical staff. In these terrifyingly lonely circumstances, millions of people across the world have died, without any recourse to their partners, relatives or friends. There have been no goodbyes, no parting words, no final embraces. Contrast this condition with other diseases, notably AIDS, where it was possible for many families and partners to be with their loved ones at the moment of death. I am reminded of Therese Frare's immortal image of the final moments in the life of HIV/AIDS activist David Lawrence Kirby. With his father holding on to David's head, almost cradling it, and members of the family grieving alongside, this image has an elegiac quality that makes one grieve every time one sees it.[53] There are no such photographs in the death archive of Covid-19 which is more like an empty vault in which memories of loved ones in the moment of death have been anaesthetized.

Against the overwhelming evidence of the erasure of death images during the pandemic, the photographs that do exist in the public domain acquire a particularly poignant significance. Arguably, for those individuals who may have lost their loved ones, these images may not even remotely compensate. They could also be oppressive reminders of the mass scale of anonymous deaths in dehumanizing conditions. Nonetheless, as documents of what happened in India between the fatal months of April and October 2021, I do believe that these photographs will remain as a powerful testament of the 'second wave', which politicians would like to erase as if nothing of consequence had happened at all.

IN THE EYES OF THE LAW

Moving beyond the affective dimensions and impact of photography, what can images of the pandemic *do* beyond documenting grief? This is where I am compelled to open what could be the hardest and least explored of investigations in dealing with the ethics of photography: the mobilization of images not merely to record but also to indict those who are responsible for any catastrophe. At the level of photography theory, this mobilization would need to be linked to the problematic of evidence. Earlier I had indicated the somewhat too-uncomplicated relationship that Barthes had established between the event being photographed

---

53 A searing account of the circumstances in which the photograph was taken with the consent of David Kirby's family and the aftermath of its circulation can be read in Ben Cosgrove, 'The Photo That Changed the Face of AIDS', *Time*, 25 November 2014: available at https://bityl.co/Av20

and its 'evidential force'.[54] For more Marxist and activist-oriented theorist-photographers like Sekula, the 'folklore of pure denotation', as ostensibly inscribed in any photograph, has the capacity to 'elevate the photograph to the legal status of document and testimonial'.[55] Developing this point in 'Counter-forensics and Photography', Thomas Keenan emphasizes that, for Sekula, a photograph's 'evidence' may be 'indexical' but it cannot be seen as 'decisive' or 'definitive'; rather, 'photographic evidence must be considered in terms of the forum or the debates into which its testimony is entered'.[56] As the very word 'forensic' implies in its Latin etymology (*forensis*), it is intrinsically linked to the idea of the 'forum' and 'the practice and skill of making an argument before a professional, political or legal gathering'.[57]

This is the fundamental premise that would need to be considered in exploring how photographs of the pandemic could be considered appropriate at a legal level in indicting those in power for their sheer negligence, if not indifference to human life.

---

54 Barthes, *Camera Lucida*, p. 89.

55 Allan Sekula, 'On the Invention of Photographic Meaning' in *Photography Against the Grain: Essays and Photo Works, 1973–1983* (London: MACK Books, 2016), p. 5.

56 Thomas Keenan, 'Counter-forensics and Photography', *Grey Room* 55 (Spring 2014): 58–77: available at https://bityl.co/BdFJ. See also, Allan Sekula, 'The Traffic in Photographs', *Art Journal* 41(1) (Spring 1981): 15–25; here p. 65. Available at: https://bityl.co/BdFf

57 This point is reiterated in Thomas Keenan and Eyal Weizman, *Mengele's Skull: The Advent of a Forensic Aesthetics* (Berlin: Sternberg Press, 2012), p. 28. In contrast to the definition of the 'forensic', 'counter-forensics', as Keenan painstakingly explains in 'Counter-forensics and Photography', in the larger context of Sekula's radical praxis, is not to be rashly associated with a dissident attempt to 'pre-emptively impede [the] future production of evidence' by consciously erasing the traces of an investigation. Rather, it has to be seen as a 'practice of "political maneuvering", as a tactical operation in a collective struggle', to appropriate forensic methods in order to work against the grain of authoritative and official institutions like the law (pp. 68–9).

Photographs in all their ontological intensity may not be able to stand up to the forensic evidence as demanded by courts of law; it is the discourse and persuasive power of the debate surrounding the photographs that could make a difference. And yet, when one probes this assumption in more concrete terms in the larger context of the pandemic in India, one is duly challenged by the protocols and technicalities of the law.

As legal scholar Jessica Silbey has cautioned in her incisive essay on 'Images in/of Law', there are any number of assumptions that need to be circumvented in order to make images, as represented in photographs and film, legally viable and verifiable.[58] The first assumption that needs to be challenged is that 'what we see' in any image is 'what we know'. In contrast, as Silbey emphasizes, for the image to also work in the eyes of the law—and not only in our own eyes as civilians: 'We need to be sure of the facts contained in the image, the relevance of the image, its perspective and potential bias, its partiality and its ambiguities.'[59] Given these exacting demands, it should come as no surprise that there is no good 'fit' between the 'inherent knowledge' contained in any image and its 'descriptive or analytical language of legal evidence and evaluation.'[60] According to Silbey, images are regarded with an innate scepticism by the law on account of their 'inscrutability', or 'mistaken total scrutability'.[61] This scepticism can be attributed at one level to the fact that advocates, judges, and juries speak 'for' images, but without the necessary training required to discern the complexity of images, which constitutes another grammar and

---

58 Jessica Silbey, 'Images in/of Law', *New York Law School Law Review* 57: 171–83.

59 Silbey, 'Images in/of Law', p. 172.

60 Silbey, 'Images in/of Law', p. 172.

61 Silbey, 'Images in/of Law', p. 172.

language. With admirable candour, Silbey observes: '[L]awyers and judges are word people and not picture people. Thinking in terms of images as building blocks for legal arguments is not how lawyers and judges are trained.'[62]

Perhaps it is not just a matter of failing to read images that lies at the core of the problem; the law has its own imperatives of discriminating between which cases are worthy of its attention and which are not worth considering. In this context, returning to Arundhati Roy's charge of a 'crime against humanity', the reality is that this charge cannot be sustained in any Indian court of law which has yet to criminalize such 'crimes' at a national level. Following the Holocaust, the charge of 'crime against humanity' was first juridically enforced during the Nuremberg trials and has since been used for those institutionally monitored atrocities by governments and states that have condoned practices like slavery and the extermination of ethnic groups. The judicial body that is most likely to assess a 'crime against humanity' would be the International Criminal Court to which India is not a signatory.

If, instead of 'crime against humanity', one focused on the charge of 'dereliction of public duty' on the basis of photographic evidence, this, too, would not be an easy charge to sustain because the protocols of the law, while admitting photographs as part of the larger search for evidence and forensic truth, still continue to have a largely ambivalent relationship with the media. As yet photographs alone are not likely to be accepted as the grounds on which judgements of 'crime' can be made, even as there are new provisions in the Indian law to accept photographs taken by a digital camera. These provisions enable ordinary citizens to serve as eyewitnesses to crimes in everyday life. Inevitably, this has

---

62 Silbey, 'Images in/of Law', p. 177.

opened a can of worms: even as digital images, unlike analog images, can be reproduced without any substantial loss to the quality of the photograph, the difficulty lies in verifying the 'original' image.[63] Such technical conundrums inevitably compli-cate issues relating to the 'authenticity' and 'accuracy' of the image: Has the light in a photograph been altered? Has it been framed differently, perhaps at the expense of excluding salient details? These considerations supplement earlier suspicions attributed to analog photography in terms of its possible 'distortion' of images through the selection of the lens, filters, the speed of the film, the length of exposure, and so on.[64]

Given these variables of photography, it becomes imperative to prove the accuracy of any image that is used within the framework of a legal procedure or court case. Without quite confronting what exactly is meant by 'accuracy', the law assumes that photographs cannot be assumed to provide evidence until they are substantially contextualized within the discursive framework of a particular argument or defence. The mere fact that the camera captures some-thing that 'happened' or 'existed' does not necessarily mean that the photograph provides actionable evidence of a 'crime.' Evidence for judicial purposes has to be *constructed* through a particular mode of argumentation in which the principle of causality between dif-ferent components of the argument has to be clearly delineated.

---

63 These issues are discussed in Aratrika Chakraborty and Anuradha Parihar, 'A Techno Legal Analysis of Admissibility of Digital Photographs as Evidence and Challenges', *International Journal of Law* 3(5) (2017): 13–18.

64 Suspicions relating to the authentication of legal evidence through pho-tography are clearly represented in Benjamin V. Madison III's article, whose title aptly sums up his scepticism: 'Seeing Can Be Deceiving: Photographic Evidence in a Visual Age—How Much Weight Does It Deserve?', *William and Mary Law Review* 25(4) (May 1984): 705–42: available at https://bityl.co/BdFy

In other words, 'evidence' has to be cogently substantiated through a verbal defence, or testimony, or eye-witness account, within the grammar of the law. While images in the form of photographs can serve to *supplement* the intent of an argument, they cannot be granted an a priori 'truth'.

Even at a supplementary level, one could ask: What kinds of photographs would qualify for the construction of legal evidence in relation to the atrocities of the pandemic? Looking back on the three images with which I began my reflections, I ask myself, somewhat rhetorically: Which of these images would 'work' in the eyes of the law? The photograph of dead bodies on the banks of the Ganga would probably be dismissed as too 'abstract'; in it, 'artistic license' in terms of the composition of the image tends to overpower the authentication of dead bodies. Likewise, the man running through funeral pyres could be rejected on grounds of being too 'sensational', apart from being far too emotionally charged. The law, it goes without saying, prioritizes rationality and restraint. The first image of the two men lying in a hospital bed with oxygen masks would probably come closest to meeting the juridical demands of factuality and an 'objective' representation of the oxygen crisis. Except that oxygen *is* being provided to the men in this image, countering the larger crime that it was denied to many other Covid-19 patients who choked to death. And yet to 'prove' this larger reality within the framework of the law, one would need to do a lot more than to invoke 'the right to life'—one would be obliged to provide actual records of the non-availability of oxygen, at specific times, in particular hospitals, to specific individuals, in a specific set of circumstances.

While it lies beyond the scope of this chapter to deal with the technicalities of law, it is perhaps more viable to think of other structures of justice that could be considered in confronting the catastrophic deaths during the 'second wave'. What if community-based truth commissions mobilized photographs and other forms of testimonial evidence on the lost lives of the pandemic? Here the focus would be not on the evidence of photographs, which are not likely to be available, but on the survivors, whose voices, stories and testimonies could be mediated by fact-finding activists and lawyers committed to seeking justice through alternative public forums.

In a bold articulation, lawyers Abhinav Verma and Radhika Roy put forward precisely this option in their pertinent article 'Why India Needs to Set Up a Truth Commission to Help It Really Heal from the Covid-19 Pandemic'.[65] Admittedly, one should acknowledge from earlier historical examples, like the South African Truth and Reconciliation Commission experiment in 'transitional justice', that the process of any truth commission is not devoid of its own limitations: the much-celebrated catharsis attributed to victims who tell their stories in public spaces can be painfully short-lived, as in any performance. Without prompt and adequate reparations, long-term dialogue and counselling, victims tend to be systematically forgotten after sharing their heartbreaking testimonials in the public domain. This leads in the long run to their disillusionment with an 'alternative' mode of authenticating justice. In some cases, the failure to receive justice in real terms can lead to post-trauma distress.[66]

---

65 Abhinav Verma and Radhika Roy, 'Why India Needs to Set Up a Truth Commission to Help It Really Heal from the Covid-19 Pandemic', *Scroll.in*, 8 March 2022: available at https://bityl.co/Av2l

66 I have elaborated at length on the promise and limitations of the South African Truth and Reconciliation process in the larger context of an 'experiment with truth' that failed on account of its bureaucratic execution and problematic granting of amnesty to perpetrators of political crimes. See my 'Countering Terror? The Search for Justice through Truth and Reconciliation', *Terror and Performance* (London, Routledge, 2014), pp. 122–47.

Despite these shortcomings in the extra legal ways of arriving at truth, I would not deny the emotional power of listening to eye-witness testimonials of survivors in accounting for the deaths of their loved ones. More critically, survivors of the dead with no possibility of receiving justice from the courts of law are likely to find some comfort through such public 'hearings'. At the very least, they can be made to recognize that they are not alone in their suffering. These hearings can also provide the ground for documenting actual cases of discrimination and death which could then serve as grounds for Public Interest Litigations. Above all, such extra-legal experiments in sharing different forms of truth-telling become necessary in order to prevent tragedies from disappearing into the oblivion of memory.

This process of forgetting is precisely what the Indian state in its present political dispensation would appear to be prioritizing in its scrupulous adherence to silence in manufacturing a form of amnesia. Simultaneously, while making sporadic attempts to politicize this silence, politicians across opposition parties in the fractious domain of Indian politics are not likely to work together to form something like an independent, non-partisan truth commission to investigate the ground realities of the Covid-19 pandemic in India. Such a commission has already been legislated in the United States, the world's most powerful democracy, whose large number of Covid-related deaths demonstrated an abysmal level of epidemiological mismanagement, fuelled by the 'America First' chauvinism of the Trump regime.[67] Clearly, such a commission is

---

67 Highlighting the fact that the death toll from the pandemic in the United States (estimated at over 1 million at the time of writing) was 'more than 200 times that of the 9/11 attacks', two Senators, Democrat Bob Menendez and Republican Susan Collins, have legislated an independent Covid-19 Commission on the lines of the 9/11 Commission, to provide Congress with 'actionable recommendations' to prevent future health crises and loss of lives. See Bob

not likely to be formed in India where ideological differences and political tensions across parties are far too intense, and the dominant political establishment would like to erase the memory of the pandemic.

Inevitably, as in the aftermath of earlier riots and human-rights abuses, it will be left to citizens' groups and coalitions of survivors to rally support for the 'crimes' inflicted on countless people who died of neglect and a collapse in public services. At the same time, I would not rule out at least some tacit support from some leading representatives of the law. From Verma and Roy's article on the need to form a truth commission in India, we learn how the Madras High Court had reprimanded the Election Commission for failing to follow Covid-19 protocols, remarking that 'officers of the Election Commission should be booked for murder'.[68] The Allahabad High Court went further by stating that the death of Covid-19 patients due to non-supply of oxygen was a 'criminal act' and no less than a 'genocide'.[69] These are very strong words coming from the courts themselves. Senior legal scholar Upendra Baxi has deftly countered charges of 'judicial overreach' in the critical statements made by diverse Chief Justices across the country:

Menendez and Susan Collins, 'There Will Be Another Pandemic: Are We Prepared For It?, *The New York Times*, 14 June 2021: available at https://-bityl.co/Av2t

   More recently, the WHO has also estimated on the basis of 'excess deaths' that India could have as many as 4.7 million deaths, a statistic that is vigorously refuted by the Indian government. See 'WHO Says Millions of Covid Deaths Went Unreported in India; Centre Questions Methodology', *The Times of India*, 5 May 2022: https://bit.ly/3lj2d9L

68 Verma and Roy, 'Why India Needs to Set Up a Truth Commission'.

69 Verma and Roy, 'Why India Needs to Set Up a Truth Commission'.

There is a murmur of dissent at such judicial articulations. We hear of 'judicial overreach', but this is pure propaganda which, unfortunately, still prevails! Constitutional courts have a judicial duty to protect and promote fundamental rights, particularly in this context [of the pandemic], the rights to liberty, life and health. It is sinister to perpetuate the 'overreach propaganda' myth when the Justices are performing their judicial duties.[70]

And yet, despite such a spirited defence of the Justices, in seeming defiance of the state, Professor Baxi does acknowledge 'the need for rectitude in judicial observations'.[71]

While it remains an open question as to how new alliances of resistance will be formed in the post-pandemic scenario, or to what extent the law can be mobilized in the larger search for justice, it becomes clear that the 'second wave' of the pandemic has left us with wounds that are not likely to heal overnight.

---

70 Upendra Baxi, 'Accelerating the "Avalanche of Evils": Towards Covid-19 Constitutionalism?', *India Legal*, 10 May 2021: available at https://bityl.co/Av30

71 Baxi, 'Accelerating the "Avalanche of Evils"'.

2.

No Time to Mourn

At a time when families have not been able to be with their loved ones at the moment of death and been prevented from participating in funeral rites and ceremonies, there is an overwhelming sense that the right to mourn has been denied. Ruptured in time, the normal concentrated period of mourning stretching over a number of days, with all the obligatory prayers, chants, all-night vigils, offerings and funerary feasts have been summarily rejected in favour of video renderings via our smartphones. Death has never seemed so far removed, so unreal, so distant and solitary, in the absence of any tangible interaction between the dead person and their family and community. All intimacy in these final moments is lost.

As a culture, we (in India) take pride in the collective modalities of coming together as families and communities during a death. It could be argued that this is no different in other parts of the world, except that the rituals of death are particularly tenacious and intricate in the Indian context, varying across class, caste and community. For an overwhelming majority of people, religious rituals tend to be meticulously observed, even if individuals in the family do not practise a particular religion. Ritual specialists and intermediaries play a key role in the ceremonies. Prevailing familial tensions tend to be temporarily suspended during the period of mourning as it becomes socially obligatory to comfort the grieving families and maintain decorum at all costs. Today, in the severe constraints imposed on our possibilities to congregate, people are separated and isolated in the aftermath of a loved one's death. Unable to comfort each other, they have no option but to fall back on their own grief in inchoate, highly personalized, untranslatable registers.

Useful as it may be to seek a binary between grief and mourning—the former appearing more privatized and locked in an interiorized state of emotions, the latter more public and exteriorized through actions and gestures—this binary could be more fluid and interactive than one imagines. As Julian Barnes points out: 'You can try to differentiate them by saying that grief is a state while mourning is a process; yet they inevitably overlap.'[1] In a more visceral register, he adds: 'Grief makes your stomach turn, snatches the breath from you, cuts off the blood supply to the brain; mourning blows in a different direction.'[2] At a visual level, one could say that grief is 'vertical—and vertiginous' as it invades one's being downwards, whereas there is a sense that the act of mourning moves horizontally and gets absorbed in the dynamics of the everyday.

This subtle interplay of grief and mourning is such that neither can be terminated with fixed deadlines. Both of them are likely to continue beyond the immediate shock of a loss or death. Certainly, it would be fatuous to assume, as psychoanalysts,

---

1 Julian Barnes, *Levels of Life* (London: Jonathan Cape, 2013), p. 88. Quoted in Guy Cools, *Performing Mourning: Laments in Contemporary Art* (Amsterdam: Valiz, Antennae-Arts in Society, 2021), p. 11.
2 In Cools, *Performing Mourning*, p. 12.

psychologists and therapists have reminded us, that one can entirely 'get over' grief. It may continue to haunt us, confound us when one least expects it. In an unexpectedly personal register, which one does not normally associate with her theoretical discourse, Judith Butler confesses that in dealing with grief,

> one is hit by waves [. . .] one starts out the day with an aim, a project, a plan [of transforming oneself through the act of mourning]. One finds oneself fallen. One is exhausted but does not know why. Something is larger than one's own deliberate plan, one's own project. [. . .] Something takes hold over you: where does it come from? [. . .] To what are we tied? By what are we seized?[3]

Butler calls attention to Freud's 'Mourning and Melancholia' (1917), where he indicates that 'we do not always know what it is *in* the person that has been lost'.[4] So, there is a profound 'enigma' in any sense of loss: 'something is hiding in the loss, something is lost within the recesses of loss'.[5] Far from being able to forget the memory of the lost one or finding some kind of substitute for what has been lost, it takes time to work through this loss in the act of mourning as one learns to live with it, sporadically, haltingly, as time passes.

SYMPTOMS OF GRIEF

Too little time has passed since the 'second wave' of the pandemic struck in India for even the beginnings of some kind of reconciliation with loss. Psychotherapists, psychologists and grief therapists

---

3 Judith Butler, *Precarious Life: The Powers of Mourning and Violence* (London and New York: Verso, 2004), p. 21.

4 Butler, *Precarious Life*, pp. 21.

5 Butler, *Precarious Life*, pp. 21–2.

working in India, who do not function in very large numbers as they do in the West, have shared how the pandemic has left some people with 'survivors' guilt'—in other words, with the feeling that 'what happened to their loved one should have happened to them instead'.[6] There is also 'compassion fatigue' which functions like a 'defence mechanism', working on the negative assumption that grief is too common and widespread to matter.[7] There are also emotions of 'helplessness' and 'anger', which are only partially addressed through the unrecognized need to open oneself to the healing power of 'shared pain' and a 'collective sort of grief'.[8]

One of the most marked symptoms of the inability to mourn has to do with the way in which the funeral or cremation can be experienced only through the mediation of technology via our smartphones. This virtualization of the 'last rites' often leaves potential mourners deeply alienated. Speaking about her dead brother in an article published in *The New York Times* titled 'At India's Funeral Pyres, Covid Sunders the Rites of Grief', Poonam Sikri, one of the persons interviewed, says, 'When I watched [my brother's] cremation on the phone, I felt a part of my body was being removed. I wanted to caress his head and rub his face and hug him one last time. I could not do that.'[9] From this statement, one realizes how the experience of watching someone's death can be dislocating, almost as if one is being amputated or dismembered at a psychic level.

---

6 Drama and movement psychotherapist Anshuma Kshetrapal, quoted in Mehta, 'Will We Ever Get Over the Grief of the Second Wave?'

7 Mehta, 'Will We Ever Get Over the Grief of the Second Wave?'

8 Psychotherapist Amrita Kajaria, quoted in Mehta, 'Will We Ever Get Over the Grief of the Second Wave?'

9 Mujib Mashal, Sameer Yasir and Shalini Venugopal Bhagat, 'At India's Funeral Pyres, Covid Sunders the Rites of Grief', *The New York Times*, 8 May 2021: available at https://bityl.co/Av3U

One also realizes how much the dimension of touch matters to people as they want to say their last goodbyes. When Sikri speaks graphically about feeling as if 'a part of her body has been removed', this can be read as part of a larger mechanization which has come to represent the alienating aftermath of experiencing death during the pandemic. In some cases, the mechanization is directly linked to the long queues for Covid-19 bodies that wait to be cremated when a slot opens up. (It is a strange grammatical construction to speak of 'bodies waiting to be cremated' but it exists because there is no family member accompanying them; they exist entirely by themselves, sealed in protective gear, in total isolation, dead.) As Mumbai-based journalist Sohini Mitter reveals: 'When my brother-in-law passed away in Kolkata, the hospital told his wife that there is a queue for cremations and "*inka number aayega*" (his number will come up). His body was kept in a morgue. Two days later at 8 a.m., the hospital called and said that he had been cremated at 3 a.m. The family didn't even get to see his face.'[10]

The anonymity of this process is brutal. And yet, as filmmaker Arkesh Ajay and media specialist Aahana Dhar have pointed out, this mechanization of a readymade discourse on sharing the death of a loved one has become ubiquitous, extending even to close friends. In this regard, they specifically point out the demor-alizing effect of receiving a WhatsApp message in which a friend states cryptically: 'My mother left me at 6 p.m. last evening.'[11] Responding critically to this objective use of words conditioned by the technological constraints of electronic communication,

---

10 Somya Lakhani and Tora Agarwala, 'How COVID-19 Replaced Rituals of Mourning with a Solitary Grief', *The Indian Express*, 16 August 2020: available at https://bityl.co/Av6y

11 Arkesh Ajay and Aahana Dhar, 'To Honour Our Dead, We Must Remember the Horror of the COVID-19 Second Wave', *The Caravan*, 6 June 2021: avail-able at https://bityl.co/Av73

they make the perceptive point: 'No one should live a life where they already have the language for grief when it arrives.'[12] Reflecting more widely on the omnipresence of grief, and its mediation through electronic bytes during the worst months of the pandemic, they add that 'no one seemed to be doing what has always been a demarcating feature of shattering grief—searching for words to express it'.[13]

In contrast to this reflexive perception of the glib mechanisms in articulating grief, we also have evidence in newspaper reports in India of young men who are completely out of their depth after losing their parents during the pandemic. One young man identified as Akhil, who is unable to come to terms with the loss of his mother, acknowledges: 'I didn't know that I would undergo grief at such a young age. No one taught me how to deal with it.'[14] Akhil is clearly in need of a grief counsellor whose profession is in short supply in India. He needs to be comforted with the chastening reminder that he may have to continue dealing with grief throughout his life. There are no quick-fix solutions or resolutions.

Unable to cope with grief, another 26-year-old man identified as Sohrab Farooqi appears to be consumed with anger: '[My mother] died due to negligence, no help reached her in time. I am so angry, I am hurt, I am broken [. . .] *Maa ke jaane ke baad kuch nahi bacha* [Nothing is left after my mother's passing]. I have suppressed my anger by working out. It helps me. I also visit her grave every Thursday.'[15] It is revealing how in the reportage of the pandemic one comes across other examples of young men dealing with anger by working out in the gym. What does it reveal?

---

12 Ajay and Dhar, 'To Honour Our Dead'.

13 Ajay and Dhar, 'To Honour Our Dead'.

14 Lakhani and Agarwala, 'How COVID-19 Replaced Rituals'.

15 Lakhani and Agarwala, 'How COVID-19 Replaced Rituals'.

More aggression on the body? Or an attempt to claim some kind of ownership and control over the self, which has been torn apart by grief?

At a more academic level, one should point out that there has been no dearth of literature around 'mental healthcare' in the Indian context of the pandemic that continues to be framed by the tenets of the Movement of Global Mental Health (MGMH).[16] How the epistemology and existing formulations of 'mental health' relate to the *suffering* of millions of people during the pandemic has yet to be addressed in a context-sensitive way. But, in one of the most recent and comprehensive critiques of MGMH and its tacit imposition of Eurocentric notions of 'mental health' on the world at large, William Sax and Claudia Lang work against the grain of its assumption that 'mental disorders' are 'clearly identifiable', measurable and quantifiable.[17] They refute the notion that mental disorders can be located in 'neurochemical processes in the brain' that can be treated with 'pharmaceutical solutions', independently of 'indigenous traditions of healing' and the comfort, however limited and fraught, of family and community.[18] Instead

---

16 From William Sax and Claudia Lang's Introduction to *The Movement for Global Mental Health: Critical Views from South and Southeast Asia* (Amsterdam: Amsterdam University Press, 2021), p. 8, we learn that, 'The Movement for Global Mental Health is a worldwide assemblage of psychiatrists, psychologists, government agencies, medical doctors, public health professionals [. . .] and others "committed to collective actions that aim to close the treatment gap for people living with mental disorders worldwide, based on two fundamental principles: evidence on effective treatments and the human rights of people with mental disorders".' The quoted lines in the second part of the sentence are from an article by Vikram Patel, Pamela Y. Collins, John Copeland, Ritsuko Kakuma, Sylvester Katontoka, Jagannath Lamichhane, Smita Naik and Sarah Skeen, 'The Movement for Global Mental Health', *British Journal of Psychiatry* 198(2) (February 2011): 88–90.

17 Sax and Lang, Introduction, p. 9.

18 Sax and Lang, Introduction, pp. 11–12.

of playing into the tenacious belief that there is a 'treatment gap' to be found in poorer, non-Western countries, they affirm the need to acknowledge a 'treatment difference' based on the fact that countries in South Asia have 'abundant resources for maintaining mental health'—resources that tend to be primitivized and, on occasion, even 'denigrated as inhumane'.[19]

Instead of the MGMH doling out what has been designated as 'packages of care' to the non-West, while advocating the need to '[scale] up services for mental and neurological disorders in low-resource settings', the MGMH, according to Sax and Lang, would be better off if it could learn to respect the local healing traditions that exist independently of the dictates of the 'pharmaceutical industry'.[20] In their ethically grounded refutation of the dominant policies by the MGMH, Sax and Lang highlight the crucial philosophical premises that the 'mind' cannot be reduced to the 'brain', still less can the 'mind' be separated from the 'body'; indeed, the larger concept of mental health cannot be separated from well-being which, in turn, needs to be embedded in the social, political, religious and economic structures of everyday life.

Against this critique provided by Sax and Lang, there is a more measured acceptance of MGMH's limitations by most institutions of psychiatry, psychology and psychotherapy in India. There is even some attempt to work against deterministic notions of 'trauma' and the 'pathologizing' of illness through a purely 'diagnostic' and 'psychiatric' approach to mental health. Instead, the growing tendency is to highlight the interplay of the biological, the psychological and the social as an appropriate methodology of dealing with mental health through what is often recognized

---

19 Sax and Lang, Introduction, pp. 14–15.
20 Sax and Lang, Introduction, p. 16, p. 26.

as a 'psychosocial approach'.[21] And yet, such is the sheer scale and intensity of the suffering faced by the estimated 150 million people afflicted by mental-health problems, that pioneering initiatives like the National Mental Health Programme, begun in 1982, and the provisions for teletherapy through online counselling services by the National Institute of Mental Health and Neuro Sciences (NIMHANS) are, at best, sources of palliative care for a predominantly middle-class constituency of beneficiaries. It is against this scenario of relative privilege that one needs to question what kind of 'care' could be made available to millions of poor and destitute people living in rural areas, whose predicament only intensified during the pandemic.

THE CASE OF RAMPUKAR PANDIT

Let us focus now on the situation faced by internal migrant workers in India, who are said to number around 100 million, and who became 'reverse migrants' after the first lockdown was imposed by the state. Attempting to address their psychological condition during the pandemic, Roli Pandey, Shilpi Kukreja and Kumar Ravi Priya ask a direct question, which they answer

---

21 In the vast body of literature on this approach where the 'social determinants' of health are given due importance, I found the following articles useful: Aparna Joshi, 'COVID-19 Pandemic in India: Through Psycho-social Lens', *Journal of Social and Economic Development* 23(Suppl. 2) (2021): 414–37: available at https://bityl.co/Av7I; Roli Pandey, Shilpi Kukreja, Kumar Ravi Priya, 'COVID-19: Mental Healthcare without Social Justice?', *Economic and Political Weekly* 55(31) (1 August 2020): 16–20; Vasundharaa S. Nair and Debanjan Banerjee, 'The Heterogeneity of Grief in India during Coronavirus Disease 2019 (COVID-19) and the National Lockdown', *Asian Journal of Psychiatry* 54 (December 2020): available at https://bityl.co/Av8R; Indira Chakravarthi and Imrana Qadeer, 'Covid-19: Reinforcing the "Technical Fix" and Distorting Public Health in India', *Economic and Political Weekly* 56(51) (18 December 2021): 13–17.

PHOTOGRAPH BY ATUL YADAV

emphatically: 'Are migrant labourers really concerned about diagnosis and treatment for PTSD [Post-traumatic Stress Disorder] or other disorders? No, they are not.'[22] Apart from their lack of access to such resources in the absence of the most rudimentary medical facilities, would the language of psychiatry be understood or easily communicated to a largely neo-literate population? Would it make any sense to them?

It would be more productive perhaps to consider a vast body of shamanic, mystical and local medical practices in India, as Sudhir Kakar had pointed out in his pioneering work *Shamans, Mystics and Doctors: A Psychological Inquiry into India and its Healing Traditions*, to which the multitude of the population in rural India turn in order to deal with diverse forms of depression and mental disturbance.[23] Arguably, even at this level, there are lacunae in addressing the harsh social, political and economic realities faced by those migrants living in cities as their temporary habitats. In a succinct report on this condition, we learn how internal migrants face 'adverse psychological consequences of multiple stresses' which, in the language of clinical psychiatry, cannot be attributed to any one set of 'emotional scars' or 'traumatic memories'.[24] Instead, they are afflicted on a daily basis by a form of habitual terror linked to everyday survival, which can be linked to 'chronic poverty, malnutrition, cultural bereavement, loss of religious practices and [community-related] social systems, malalignments

---

22 Pandey et al., 'COVID-19: Mental Healthcare without Social Justice?'

23 Sudhir Kakar, *Shamans, Mystics and Doctors: A Psychological Inquiry into India and Its Healing Traditions* (New Delhi: Oxford University Press, 2012). First published in 1982, it remains a vital point of reference in attempting to find local and indigenous resources of healing outside a Eurocentric 'medicalization' of the body.

24 Ranjana Choudhari, 'COVID 19 Pandemic: Mental Health Challenges of Internal Migrant Workers of India', *Asian Journal of Psychiatry* 54 (December 2020): available at https://bityl.co/Av8e

with a new culture, coping with language difficulties', all of which contribute to their precarity and vulnerability at material levels, both social and physical.[25] To address, however inadequately, the depth of suffering faced by internal migrants during the pandemic, one has no other option but to keep in mind the oppressively 'normal' conditions that constituted their lives in pre-pandemic times.

Keeping this oppressive 'normal' in mind, I will now focus on what could be regarded as an archetypal image of a construction worker during the pandemic—40-year-old Rampukar Pandit, who was seen sobbing on Nizamuddin Bridge in the Delhi–Uttar Pradesh border, around 1,400 kilometres away from his home in Begusarai, Bihar. In a photograph that has circulated widely, Pandit is seen clutching his mobile phone. His face is a picture of grief, the veins in his forehead protruding, his mouth open in anguish, as he takes in some terrible news on the phone. In this photograph by Atul Yadav which went viral shortly after it was taken on 17 May 2021, we learn that it captures the moment when Pandit learnt from his wife in the village that their son, who was not yet a year old, had died. It is additionally poignant to note that the father had never seen his son because he was too busy earning a living in Delhi on a construction site. Now, stuck on Nizamuddin Bridge, he pleads with the police to allow him to go home, 'Will a father not want to go home and even mourn the death of his son with his family?' To this request, the policeman retorts: 'Will your son come alive if you go back home? This is lockdown, you can't move.'[26]

---

25 Choudhari, 'COVID 19 Pandemic'.

26 'Coronavirus Lockdown: Image of a Weeping Rampukar Pandit Becomes Symbol of India's Migrant Worker Tragedy', *The Hindu*, 17 May 2020: available at https://bityl.co/Av8l

This snapshot of Pandit's predicament is too cruel for words. It is another matter that he was ultimately rescued by a social worker who managed to get him a ticket on a special train back to Begusarai; he got home, but only after spending a harrowing time in a quarantine centre. In talking about his grief, Pandit uses words and expressions that capture its intensity with a physical force: he speaks of being struck by a 'bolt of lightning' when he hears the news of his son's death. In an equally graphic register at a later stage of his loss, he says, '*Dukh itna hai jaise chhaati pe chattaan rakh diya hai kisi ne*' (The pain was like a boulder crushing my chest). But, immediately after, he adds, '*Upar se kaam nahi hai, na paisa*' (On top of that, there is no work or money).[27]

I highlight this observation because it gets to the heart of trying to understand the complexities of finding an adequate language for grief in the context of migrant labour in India. Clearly, any theory of mental health that has been nurtured in a European context needs to be substantially revised and translated within the socioeconomic immediacies of the Indian context. One would need to question if such a revision or translation is viable at all. In Europe, the psychiatric focus is invariably on 'the traditionally unified subject', who is, more often than not, from an educated middle-class social background, who submits to a certain course of medical treatment over a period of time. Of particular importance in this process is the use not just of pharmaceuticals but also of words shared with the medical practitioner, more often than not in the pandemic through the ostensibly 'innovative' mode of teletherapy. This form of communication is being favoured even by those counsellors and grief therapists in India who are aware of the effectivity of person-to-person communication in a more intimate, tactile and trusting relationship between counsellor

---

27 Lakhani and Agarwala, 'How COVID-19 Replaced Rituals'.

and patient. However, expediency and a false sense of 'tele-efficiency'—generated through a template questionnaire—tend to overpower any serious acknowledgement of the limitations of technology.[28] As for the crucial role played by *silence* in Indian contexts of grief and mourning, where the person afflicted by suffering may not wish to speak at all, or may use silence as a form of protest or self-protection, this has yet to be fully factored into the healing processes of migrants.[29]

Without attempting to analyse Pandit's predicament in psychiatric terms, I would re-inflect the formulation of 'life vs livelihood' that has been somewhat oppressively reiterated in the discourse around the pandemic in India. This formulation, which is presented as an 'either-or' construction, underlines the point that if people don't die of the coronavirus, they are more likely to die of hunger. In a less formulaic manner, Pandit makes us think of 'pain' and 'poverty' as inextricably linked, compelling us to confront the simple but critical point that it is not just the psychological manifestations of grief that are of concern but also its economics. Along with *dukh*, which could translate as sorrow or pain, there is the absence of *kaam* (work) and *paisa* (money). In

---

28 The role of tele-counselling is documented at length with much statistical detail in Joshi, 'COVID-19 Pandemic in India: through Psycho-social Lens'. Her case-study is iCALL, 'a national level technology assisted psycho-social counselling service and field action project of the Tata Institute of Social Sciences, India', operating in 10 different languages. While there is much evidence in Joshi's article about the disillusionment of the callers with the public health system, and a tacit acknowledgement that technology is not a 'panacea for all mental health issues', there is no self-reflexive critique of iCALL's limitations in addressing the grievances of people. The quantification of data overwhelms qualitative analysis.

29 Drawing on the writings of Veena Das, notably *Life and Words: Violence and the Descent into the Ordinary* (Berkeley and Los Angeles: University of California Press, 2007), I have written about different gradations and epistemologies of silence as experienced by victims of terror and communal riots in my book *Terror and Performance*, pp. 135–9.

addition to the pain suffered from the death of a child, one is forced to confront the enduring pain of unemployment and poverty. Compassion for the plight of migrants like Pandit needs to be supplemented by a strong awareness of the socioeconomic injustice that dominates their lives. Unless this injustice is confronted, all attempts to arrive at 'minimal mental healthcare' are likely to be of little use. It is not the assumed absence of 'mental health' in India but the recognition of social suffering that needs to be put on the agenda.

From what little we know of Rampukar Pandit, we can be sure that his livelihood as a labourer in the city has been seriously jeopardized because he resists the possibility of coming back. In this, he is one among a growing number of migrant workers who have been reluctant to resume their former work in a city which provided them with no support or comfort in their hour of need. The desperate hope of receiving some kind of financial assistance 'on compassionate grounds' from state governments also remains unfulfilled. Pandit is likely to be forgotten as he continues to wait for help and his grief gets neutralized by the necessary task of survival—he does not have the luxury to mourn as he struggles to exist. In the process, his grief is likely to deepen or else be numbed into a resigned silence.

LIVING WITH THE DEAD

In order to more fully understand the impact of the disruption of death rituals, it would be useful to describe what goes into their performance. Without attempting to generalize about all communities, which would be an impossible and highly reductive endeavour, I draw on an extended series of observations made by folklorist and oral historian Komal Kothari in the context of his father's death rituals, following the time-tested practices of the Oswal Jain community in Jodhpur, Rajasthan.[30] While the details that I narrate here from my book *Rajasthan: An Oral History* (2003) are specifically related to this particular sub-caste of the Jain community, they resonate among other Jain and Hindu communities as well, though of course with the inevitable variations, additions and deletions. I should also point out that my focus here is on the physical actions that go into the performance of one set of funerary practices, without any attempt to 'universalize' the complex religious and metaphysical significances and differences that exist across different cultural understandings of death. This would require a different narrative.[31]

In Kothari's account, the ritual practices of death begin with the smearing of *gobar* (cow dung) or *ganga jal* (holy water of the Ganga) or *gaumutra* (cow urine) on the ground where the body is to be placed. Bathing the body is done according to strict rules based on who has the right to do so. Thereafter, the clothing of the body will depend on whether the dead person has left behind which clothes he or she wishes to wear (in Kothari's case, his father had discreetly indicated the clothes he wished to wear for his cremation). The cloth for the *kafan* (shroud) has to be bought from specialized shops, along with other more intimate clothing items. For instance, as Kothari had pointed out to me, when his brother-in-law from Udaipur died, it was the family custom that 'the *chaddi* [underwear] should be red and that [. . .] a thin cotton mattress [be] placed on the bier'. All these details are known not only to

30 Bharucha, *Rajasthan*, pp. 133–6.
31 See, for instance, the learned reflections of Purushottama Bilimoria, 'Hindu Response to Dying and Death in the Time of COVID-19', *Frontiers in Psychology* 12 (2021)—available at https://bityl.co/Av9b—which essentialize 'Hindu' rituals and eschatologies of death without problematizing the considerable differences that exist across Hindu belief systems and socioeconomic contexts in relation to caste, class and region.

some members of the family but also to those cloth dealers and shopkeepers specializing in funerary services. The latter are fully informed about the sartorial minutiae of the dead, cutting across castes and sub-castes, each of which require a different funerary attire and accoutrements. Following the dressing of the dead body for its final journey, there are rules regarding how it should be carried to the cremation ground, with attention paid to placement: at which end the head, at which the feet. Likewise, the cry or chant of the pallbearers—this could vary from region to region, from one caste group to another.

At the cremation ceremony itself, it is the eldest son who leads, circumambulating the dead body on the dry wood pyre, following the instructions of the priest in his performance of the last rites. Each gesture, chant and offering prior to the lighting of the pyre has a performative intensity, each detail not merely invoked but embodied through the 'doing' of the ritual, where gestures and actions are followed by repetition. What unfolds in the last rites is a re-enactment of what has been prescribed and practised for generations—a fixed script and sequence of gestures in a codified choreography. Nothing can be out of place. This last ritual, which is enacted on behalf of a dead person, has to follow the rules, with no false notes or careless gestures. In a sense, it could be said that the mourners and cremators are not 'performing' the ritual—rather, it is the ritual that 'performs' itself through an enactment of its rules.

Following the cremation, there are more rituals beginning with the task of collecting the bones and ashes of the dead. As Kothari specifies, they are gathered in a red *theli* (bundle) for women and a white one for men. Specifically kept outdoors or in a temple near the cremation ground, these ashes remain outside the home until they are deposited in a river or water body. Invariably, all these solemn instances of parting with the dead culminate in a feast which brings the family and community together. Here again there are different rules regarding the food to be served. In the case of the Oswal Jain community, Kothari pointed out that the food had to be specially prepared and sent from the in-laws' house—bitter food (*kaduwa kava*), as it is called. Accompanying these funerary rites and rituals are in-house social events—for instance, the *ratijaga*, or all-night sessions in which women chant songs with a ritualistic content, referring to dead ancestral figures, some of whom continue to haunt as spirits.

In the labyrinthine intricacy of these rituals, what needs to be kept in mind is not just the density of the performative details, which have been 'memorized' at a corporeal level, but also the intense *intimacy* of what goes into commemorating the dead and parting with the dead body. The key point that Kothari emphasized to me over and over again in our conversations is that the dead are regarded *as if they are still alive* for as long as the funeral is taking place. Indeed, this intimacy with the dead can continue until the ashes are eventually deposited in a water body—in a nearby river or else, if one had the time or financial resources, at a more sacred pilgrimage site like Varanasi or Haridwar. In words that I continue to remember with an odd sense of comfort, this is what Kothari had shared with me about the last journey:

> When you go to Haridwar to immerse the remains of the dead (called *phul*, or flowers), there are other rituals that need to be followed. If four people, for instance, are going to Haridwar for the final rites of a dead person, they will buy five tickets. After all, one of their relatives is travelling with them. If they order tea or food, they will always order for five persons. [. . .] However, when they return home, they will only buy four tickets. By this time they will have requested the Bhairava of Ganga, Lord Shiva's attendant, to

accompany them so that the person whose *phul* have been immersed in Hardwar will not return home with them.[32]

At one level, this narrative evokes how gently and persuasively one lets go of the dead. However, it does not preclude the fact that the dead *can* return if their spirits have not been appeased, or if they wish to be commemorated through the construction of a particular shrine. There is an entirely different set of rituals for the appeasement of the dead who come alive in shamanic ceremonies, during which a dead person returns in spirit to speak through the *bhopa's* (shaman-priest) body and voice. This is another set of rituals that I cannot elaborate on here.[33]

Suffice it to say, as Kothari emphasized, 'In all the hundreds of little things that happen after a person dies, you continue to treat the dead as a living being [. . .] Now, to my mind, if you are capable of treating a dead person as a living being immediately after his or her death, then he or she can live for eternity. The dead can be with you forever.'[34] This is a simple way of suggesting what psychoanalysts have analysed in more technical terms—of internalizing the dead through the process of 'incorporation' instead of severing ties or seeking a 'substitute' for them. Kothari does not use this vocabulary, but he makes us see how a dead body can be a living being, with the suggestion that the dead can continue to live within ourselves.

However, to complicate matters, keeping in mind the disruption of rituals during the pandemic, what if the funeral rites and rituals, as described above, cannot be practised, and the dead body is not physically present to be washed and touched and embraced? What then? Here I cannot fall back on Kothari to provide an

32 Bharucha, *Rajasthan*, p. 135.
33 Bharucha, *Rajasthan*, pp. 130–2.
34 Bharucha, *Rajasthan*, p. 136.

answer because, perhaps fortuitously, he passed away many years ago, and in all the hundreds of hours of conversation that I had with him over three years, we never once addressed anything on the scale of a pandemic even as we addressed droughts and famines at a regional level. I am not entirely sure how he would have reacted to this moment that we are living today. However, I speculate that it would have been a moment of deep sorrow for him were he unable to participate in the death rituals of any of his family or community members.

This came through sharply in his conversation with me when he recalled a friend's bereavement in France. This particular friend had communicated to Kothari that her father had died but he could not be buried because there was no space in the local cemetery to accommodate his body. So, for eleven days and nights, the body remained in a morgue, after which it was removed, and the family settled for a burial in the cemetery once a plot was made available. In responding to this situation, which has nothing to do with the accumulation of bodies in a pandemic but was, merely, an instance of a cemetery not having enough space—a mere bureaucratization of mortuary services—I still remember how Kothari was totally bewildered that such a delayed funeral could be accepted as 'normal'. What would he have said about the phenomenon of 'delayed funerals' in the context of the pandemic today? I can only believe that his bewilderment would have deepened.

PERFORMING MOURNING: LIFE AND ART

From the description of ritual actions and gestures surrounding death, it becomes obvious that death in the Indian context is a highly charged community event in which mourners participate actively. Psychosomatic symptoms of distress, anger and a feeling of helplessness are likely to emerge when people are prevented from 'performing' the act of mourning, which they would regard as a fundamental right, a means of deepening their relationality to the lost person.

To provide another vivid testimony of what has been lost during the pandemic in terms of mourning a person's death, let me turn to an example that comes from a Christian background in the North-East Indian state of Mizoram. The speaker is Margaret Zama, a professor of English, who has never missed a single funeral in two decades of living in Aizawl's Chawlhhmun locality. With the lockdown, however, she has had to face the social and cultural aberration of not attending even one. In a report of her predicament, we can begin to understand not so much her personal sense of loss but the erasure of a larger vibrant sociality that can be said to constitute the community's habitus:

> Death in Mizoram is rarely a private affair. 'Mizo funerals are not just attended by relatives, friends and acquaintances but by complete strangers too,' says Zama. When someone dies in Mizoram, loudspeaker announcements (*tlangau*) are made to inform the entire locality and the Young Mizo Association (ZMA)—the most influential organization in the state—swings into action to make arrangements for the funeral. Everyone in the neighbourhood participates, whether it is to build a coffin, dig the grave, cook for the family, or sit together and sing funeral songs through the night. In the post-COVID world, the funerals are shorter and only a few participate—rituals have been cut short or done away with.[35]

This description gets to the heart of the communal festivity that can animate a funeral, where the sociality of death comes alive in a heartening way. It becomes clear from this account that death

---

35 Lakhani and Agarwala, 'How COVID-19 Replaced Rituals'.

is not meant to be mourned in solitude but, rather, celebrated with community participation and fervour.

I would hold on to this basic point to say that 'performing mourning', which is the title of an engrossing and self-reflexive book by dance dramaturg Guy Cools, has very different manifestations in the Indian context as opposed to the profuse examples of Euro-American artists *performing* the act of mourning on stage and in visual installations.[36] These performances are meticulously documented in Cools' narrative with a perceptible empathy. After reading his book in the thick of the pandemic, I was compelled to write to him because, in my dramaturgical experience, I would have to say that there are almost no examples that I can think of in the Indian theatrical context where individual performers have enacted their own losses on stage in an explicitly autobiographical mode. This is not to say that 'mourning' as a theme or a trope or a provocation does not exist in Indian theatre. But, to reiterate my point, it would be hard to find any body of work in contemporary Indian theatre and dance where the performance itself on stage can be regarded as an act of mourning in a self-consciously autobiographical enactment of grief and loss.

How then does one account for the fact that there is such a profusion of solo performances in Europe and America where artists feel compelled to enact their personal losses on stage or through an artwork? Could it be related to the fact that the rituals surrounding death in communitarian contexts have been denied to these artists or attenuated over the years, leaving them with the need to find their own ways of mourning a loved one through highly individuated modes of performance? In a generous response to my questions, Cools supported my tentative hypothesis that the

---

36 Cools, *Performing Mourning*.

profusion of artistic representations of mourning in the Euro-American context could be a symptomatic response to the relative *absence* of time-tested rituals of mourning in everyday life.[37]

Indeed, Cools' entire body of writing and work as a dramaturg on mourning can be seen as a means of confronting—and transforming—the denial of mourning in public life that he has had to live with for most of his life. In a profoundly personal register, he shares his traumatic experience as an 11-year-old when he was prevented from attending his father's funeral. Over the years, he has learnt to live with this trauma and situate it within a larger historical context. This is how he attempts to explain the context in *Performing Mourning*:

> Our Western society has suppressed external rituals. It has interiorized mourning, which carries serious risks of psychological, physical, and energetic blockages in the body. Through cyclically revisiting one's mourning, grief is eventually exteriorized and exorcized, resulting in the loosening of negative energy or energy blockages. In the process, personal experiences are integrated into a larger collective tradition and can become material for a creative practice. Artistic practices can open up spaces for articulating and renegotiating the pain of loss.[38]

---

37 Correspondence with author, 21 May 2021.

38 Cools, *Performing Mourning*, p. 51. Emphasizing that 'the liminal state of an as yet unresolved mourning process [. . .] is often better expressed through artistic expression than through psychological terminology' (p. 57), Cools calls attention to one of the central premises in Peggy Phelan's *Mourning Sex: Performing Public Memories* (London and New York: Routledge, 1997), namely, that 'theatre and performance respond to a psychic need to rehearse for loss, and especially for death' (p. 3). However, one needs to keep in mind that this 'psychic need', for Phelan, is located prior to the learning of 'specific vocabularies of grief'—as, for instance, through performance—insofar as 'the human subject is born ready to mourn', at that very moment when it

Whether grief can be 'exorcized' even as it is externalized, or whether 'energy blockages' are directly linked to grief, are details that could be more deeply questioned at psychological and psychoanalytical levels. However, the thrust of Cools' categorical statement about the suppression of external rituals does make sense in a larger 'Western' context where, as literary theorist Tammy Clewell, in her reflections on 'mourning beyond melancholia', points out, 'The medicalization of illness and dying in the closing decades of the nineteenth century not only rendered death an increasingly taboo subject; it also contributed to the disappearance of Victorian mourning customs and to [. . .] the demonizing of all social displays of bereavement.'[39] One of the many achievements of Freud, according to Clewell, was his resistance to 'this cultural repression of loss' in his seminal understanding of mourning as 'a necessary labor, theorizing the psyche as an internal space for grief work [Trauerarbeit], and bring a discussion of bereavement into the public domain.'[40]

In a more explicit historical register, one could link the absence of mourning in the Euro-American context with the mass anonymization of death through the large number of casualties suffered during the First World War and the Spanish flu pandemic. In these mass casualties, the dead ceased to matter as

is '[s]evered from the placenta and cast from the womb' (p. 5). It is this pre-existing 'syntax of loss' which is 'hard-wired into the psyche' that enables one to cope with loss. In its absence, 'life-as-loss' would be 'unbearable' (p. 5).

39 Tammy Clewell, 'Mourning Beyond Melancholia: Freud's Psychoanalysis of Loss', *Journal of the American Psychoanalytic Association*, 52(1) (2004): 43–67. The 'demonizing of social displays of bereavement' is drawn from Geoffrey Gorer, *Death, Grief, and Mourning* (New York: Arno Press, 1977), p. 128. I am grateful to Dr Amrita Narayanan for recommending Clewell's text and for clarifying some fundamental shifts in Freud's understanding of mourning from 'Mourning and Melancholia' (1917) to 'The Ego and the Id' (1923).

40 Clewell, 'Mourning Beyond Melancholia', p. 44.

individuals who could be mourned with appropriate rituals. As the quantification of dead bodies became a reality to deal with, accompanied by the stigmatization of their possible infection, it was almost inevitable that death became more business-like, almost impersonal, driven by pragmatic concerns of disposing of dead bodies in open graves. This is certainly the case in our times, cutting across different parts of the world, where the pandemic has terminated the possibilities of allowing the performance of mourning to be personally felt and experienced through pre-scribed death rituals. Now, as highlighted earlier in this section, ad hoc funereal practices have been prioritized on an expedient basis with scant respect for the grief of the families. This opens up questions whether there are other ways of mourning that are not necessarily mediated by the existence of death-related rituals. How does one mourn when rituals are disrupted? Can one mourn at all? Or does one need rituals in the first place?

'ARTISTIC' MOURNING PRACTICES

At this point, it would be useful to shift the focus from the crisis facing the disruption in rituals of mourning to more personal enactments of death, grief and mourning in performance and the visual arts. If in the earlier section I have dealt with mourning (or the inability to mourn) in the larger context of ritual practice, social behaviour and the cultures of everyday life, I will turn now to tra-ditions of artistic practice which come with their own grammars, aesthetics and the right to create narratives around mourning that are performed on stage or in a museum space. These performances are self-consciously framed within specific institutional contexts for audiences that are, to a large extent, familiar with or open to multiple experiences of 'artistic mourning'. Inevitably, the con-text that I focus on is European, a significant contrast to Indian representations of mourning in fiction and performance (which will be addressed later in this chapter).

For European representations of mourning as performance, I draw some of my evidence from Cools' study which offers a panorama of examples of how mourning can be performed on stage and in site-specific spaces with a deeply embodied subjectivity and self-reflexive awareness. Many of these solo performances are not likely to be known outside an Euro-American context and some of them are exclusively European; they could be regarded as 'minor' works using the word in a Deleuzian sense to mark the power of the marginal against all forms of majoritarianism.[41] To mourn, one does not necessarily have to submit to spectacle or elaborate productions; even the smallest of improvisations can qualify as an act of mourning and, indeed, could be more intimate and powerful than spectacular representations.

In this regard, Cools calls attention to solo acts of mourning in which individual performers mourn for the loss of a friend, the death of unborn children, even nonhuman objects like a drum which could be disappearing in the larger context of a specific indigenous performance culture.[42] In Cools' brief description of these enactments, it becomes clear that these are intense works whose dimensions of mourning are steeped in a somatic psychophysical immediacy which needs to be experienced at a phenomenological level, the spectator tuning into each moment of the enactment with critical empathy. While such performances cannot be meaningfully evoked without being experienced, I turn to those acts in the public domain which have been recorded on video. In this format, I engage with embodied performances in

---

41 Félix Guattari and Gilles Deleuze, *Kafka: Toward a Minor Literature* (Dana Polan trans.) (Minneapolis: University of Minnesota Press, 1986).

42 Cools, *Performing Mourning*, p. 96, pp. 142–3, p. 132.

different installations within the larger framework of exhibitions, whose recordings can be accessed on YouTube and other websites. Today, as websites and electronic networks have become extensions of the museum, one is in a somewhat better position to examine the ambivalences of what happens to performances of mourning when they are recorded and 'exhibited', both within the framework of the museum and within the more intimate environs of one's computer at home.

One such performance site that offers an unusual body of evidence relating to artworks of mourning is the exhibition *Trauern: Von Verlust und Veränderung* [Mourning: On Loss and Change] at the Hamburger Bahnhof Museum, Berlin. This was one of the first major exhibitions that opened serendipitously in February 2020 around the same time as the pandemic was beginning to spread in Europe and the rest of the world. Drawing on the art works themselves and supplemented by Brigitte Kolle's curatorial framework and the text of Inga Dreesen's catalogue, I will extrapolate three motifs from this exhibition—artifice, objects and the documentary. I will also consider what happens when mourning is transformed into an artistic 'spectacle' by focusing on an installation which was not shown in the *Trauern* exhibition. While these motifs may seem to interrupt the flow of this particular narrative through their inscription of Euro-American artistic mourning practices, I believe that they offer valuable points of reference in highlighting and complicating the assumptions relating to mourning as it gets transformed through art practices in the Indian context.

Artifice

In experiencing an art work of mourning within the framework of a museum, one is inevitably compelled to engage with the ambivalence of the experience. On the one hand, one can respond to the art work as a manifestation of authentic feeling and grief. On the other hand, one cannot help being struck by the artifice with which the art work is framed at implicit or explicit levels. Far from neutralizing the experience of grief, it could be argued that the artifice framing the video or the installation has the capacity to 'contain' the emotion and thereby heighten its impact.[43] Simultaneously, the artifice can also succeed in compelling the viewer to engage with grief in a reflexive manner. The fact that the representation of grief is not unequivocally 'real' makes the act of witnessing it all the more challenging at a hermeneutic level.

A strong example of 'implicit' artifice can be traced, however nebulously, in Dutch conceptual and performance artist Bas Jan Ader's video-performance from the early 1970s titled *I'm Too Sad to Tell You*.[44] In this performance piece, we see the artist weeping before the camera, at first almost involuntarily, then building towards a paroxysm of sobs, his entire body seized by emotion. At one level, what registers here is the politics of watching a man weep in public, which works against norms of masculinity in heteronormative understandings of gender. On the other hand, feminist critics like Jennifer Doyle have argued that Ader's performance can be perceived as 'real' precisely because it works in

---

43 Cools emphasizes that it is the stylization of 'forms' created by artists to perform mourning that results in 'a certain artifice'. It is this artifice that is in a position 'to contain and (to an extent) control the grief' (p. 167).

44 A recording of *I'm Too Sad to Tell You* can be seen on https://ytube.io/3PrV. This is one among several versions of the performance. For a brief history of how the performance evolved and assumed different forms, see the Wikipedia entry for *I'm Too Sad to Tell You*.

the tradition of the 'melancholy white male artist'. If a woman had to weep in a similar manner, she would be regarded as 'either acting or in hysterics'.[45] Dutch journalist Betty van Garrel put it in an even more acerbic register: 'Ader is a sentimental loser, a romantic softie, a problem case and not even original in that.'[46]

In a more sympathetic register, the catalogue of the *Trauern* exhibition asks: Is the scene performed by Ader 'authentic' or 'playacted'? Is the artist 'feeling deep sorrow due to a specific loss, or is he in a state of ecstasy?'[47] Clearly, given the range of these responses, there is an enigmatic quality to the performance that compels one to interpret the act of crying in different critical modes. Given its relentless intensity, the act, I would submit, cannot be dismissed as mere indulgence; it is too raw and visceral not to register as an emotionally affecting experience, even as it is hard to spell out why one is so inexplicably moved on watching it.

A more 'explicit' form of artifice that frames the performance of mourning is almost flaunted in the blatantly synthetic performance of Icelandic artist, Ragnar Kjartansson, cheekily titled *God* (2007).[48] 'Hot pink', in the words of the catalogue, the setting of this musical video is monochromatic in its strident 'pink-ness', almost bordering on gay camp. Against an overwhelming background of pink curtains, surrounded by a chamber orchestra including harp, drums, double bass, piano, string and wind instruments,

---

45 Doyle's position, as expressed in her book *Hold It Against Me: Difficulty and Emotion in Contemporary Art* (Durham: Duke University Press, 2013) is included in the Wikipedia entry on Ader's performance.

46 Included in the Wikipedia entry on *I'm Too Sad to Tell You*.

47 Booklet of *Trauern: Von Verlust und Veränderung* [Mourning: On Loss and Change], Hamburger Bahnhof Museum, Berlin, February 2020. See https://bityl.co/AvAC, exhibit #5.

48 Kjartansson's performance can be watched on Vimeo: https://vimeo.com/292676427

Kjartansson, dressed in a black suit and black bow tie, his blond hair slicked back, sings just one sentence in a dreamy melodic voice—'Sorrow conquers happiness'—in a never-ending loop. When I first saw the performance on video (via Vimeo), I was not sure whether I should laugh at its 'tongue-in-cheek irony', as the catalogue points out, or whether the sheer repetition of the voice crooning the disturbing home-truth of sorrow conquering happiness should numb me into silence.[49]

While in the performance by Ader, there is a strong personal core to the grief, even as it is not clear for whom Ader is crying—is he crying for himself?—the second performance by Kjartansson moves more directly into the realm of theatricality where it is not easy to sense any personal loss animating the performance. Even so, the sheer repetition of what has been described as Kjartansson's 'endurance-based art' results in an opulent hauntology of grief. The setting of the performance may have all the glitter of a televised music show in whose ambience grief is commodified for the global market. And yet, for all its irony, the ceaseless refrain 'Sorrow conquers happiness' plays on the nerves with a mordant wit and contributes to the *affect* of sharing a collective grief.

Objects

At a more quotidian level, mourning is often commemorated through loving evocations of objects left behind by a dead person. Highlighting images of a cigarette lighter, a camera, a lipstick, a hairbrush, a scarf, sunglasses, a perfume atomizer and slippers, artist Jennifer Loeber inventories the everyday objects used by her dead mother in a simple, yet evocative diptych of photographs titled *Left Behind* (2014).[50] On the left side of the screen, we see

---

49 Booklet of *Trauern*, exhibit #6.
50 *Left Behind* can be viewed at http://www.jenniferloeber.com

images of Loeber's mother from the family photograph album before she was diagnosed with cancer; on the right, we see the personal objects that she has left behind.

Without using the language of psychoanalysis, the artist shares the intention of her work as a personal attempt to move from melancholia to a state of being in which her mourning could be shared with a wider public.

> When my Mom died suddenly in 2013, I found myself overwhelmed by the need to keep even the most mundane of her belongings. But instead of providing comfort, they became a source of deep sadness and anxiety. The only way I could imagine moving past it all was to focus on how to interact with these objects cathartically.
>
> In 2014, I quietly debuted this body of work on Instagram to diminish my own sentimentality and to reframe what exactly my Mom left behind. Each photograph is paired with an archival image that ultimately speaks to its subject.[51]

As much as the objects speak to us in all their 'mundanity', as Loeber puts it, what remains more enigmatic and haunting are the images of the dead mother from the family album. These images are presented without any captions. All we see are different stills of a woman posing against scenic backdrops during a holiday, smoking a cigarette on the balcony, playing with her children, sitting at the kitchen table, welcoming a guest during Christmas, standing against a tree with autumnal colours. Each of these images, as Loeber puts it bluntly, 'ultimately speaks to its subject': the adverb is precise—'ultimately', in the final analysis. In whose eyes do these images resonate most meaningfully?

---

51 Prefatory statement by Jennifer Loeber included on her website.

Here one has no other option but to return to Barthes and the way in which he consumed, protected and transfigured the images of his mother, which 'ultimately' spoke only to him. He speaks most luminously about what he calls the 'Winter Garden Photograph', which he claims 'exists only for me. For you, it would be nothing but an indifferent picture, one of the thousand manifestations of the "ordinary" [...]. At most, it would interest your studium: period, clothes, photogeny; but, in it, for you, no wound.'[52]

The significance of these words in the context of Loeber's photographic project is that, far from excluding the 'ordinary' (which is anathema to Barthes), she in fact engages with it. But if one examines her images more closely, it becomes obvious that there are different gradations of the 'ordinary': On the one hand, there is the 'ordinary' of everyday household objects belonging to a woman; on the other, there is the 'ordinary' of a mother's everyday life, which remains elusive and yet so deeply significant that, in the final analysis, it exists only for the artist herself.

In words whose resonance is immeasurable, and in response to which no explanation or critical gloss is necessary, Barthes adds:

> Time eliminates the emotion of loss (I do not weep), that is all. For the rest, everything has remained motionless. For what I have lost is not a Figure (the Mother), but a being; and not a being, but a *quality* (a soul): not the indispensable, but the irreplaceable. I could live without the Mother (as we all do, sooner or later); but what life remained would be absolutely and entirely *unqualifiable* (without quality).[53]

---

52 Barthes, *Camera Lucida*, p. 73.
53 Barthes, *Camera Lucida*, p. 75.

Documentary

Through the tropes of 'artifice' and 'objects', I have provided a few glimpses of how mourning can be *performed* at personal levels in a Euro-American context of contemporary art practice. It would be hard to find such self-conscious expressions of grief and mourning in the Indian artistic sector where autobiographical renderings of loss are not readily found even as loss can be visualized as a theme or trope or concept. One should emphasize at this point that not all the artworks on mourning as represented in the *Trauern* exhibition were as explicitly personal as the examples that I have addressed above. Indeed, some of the most striking work in the exhibition was documentary in nature—for instance, the Albanian film and performance artist Adrian Paci's video work titled *Interregnum* (2017).[54]

In this assemblage of film and televisual footage of public mourning, Paci juxtaposes images from 'the state television archives of communist dictatorships—from Europe to Asia, from Stalin's funeral service to Mao's'.[55] Significantly, he consciously excludes images of the dead rulers and dictators, close-ups of coffins, long shots of military parades, along with 'specific temporal and spatial markers that might distinguish each historical event'.[56] Instead, as Richard Birkett points out in his striking analysis of *Interregnum* within the larger framework of the 'politics of memory', Paci constructs an intricate montage of images through which he projects an 'imaginary of a collective transnational and

---

54 While the full footage of *Interregnum* is not available, some glimpses of the powerful images in this video artwork are available at https://fbook.cc/3nWf and https://ytube.io/3PrW

55 Booklet of *Trauern*, exhibit #3.

56 Richard Birkett, 'A Politics of Memory: On Adrian Paci's "Interregnum"' (2017), *Mousse Magazine*, 1 October 2021: available at https://bityl.co/AvAY

transhistorical scenography of mourning' in which the archetypal figure of 'the people' takes 'center stage'.[57] Through families clustering around the radio to hear the announcement of the leader's death to long lines of mourners 'stoically waiting to pay their respects', Paci creates a panorama of people mourning the loss of the leader. Significantly, while this would seem to play into a mass anonymity of grief, the power of the work lies in Paci's ability to capture 'a complexity of individual emotional expressions, from hysterical and body-shaking grief to faces frozen in apparent resignation'.[58] Here again, as in performance artist Ader's more personally self-enacted performance of grief addressed earlier, it is hard to say whether the public is truly grieved by the loss of dictators like Stalin and Mao, or whether grief has been so manipulated by the technologies of propaganda that it becomes another kind of state-determined performance.

Against this conundrum, the Russian artist Aslan Goisum's austere yet deeply moving documentary-video-performance *People of No Consequence* (2016), also exhibited at the *Trauern* exhibition, focuses on 119 elderly Chechen survivors of enforced deportation under the Soviet regime, who are from 73 to 105 years of age.[59] What is on display is the actual physical presence of the survivors who take around 8 minutes and 34 seconds to assemble in a bare room with chairs placed in horizontal rows and a Soviet-style painting of urban development in the background. The survivors sit and stare directly into the camera in silence. It is we as witnesses

---

57 Birkett, 'A Politics of Memory'.

58 Birkett, 'A Politics of Memory'.

59 Booklet of *Trauern*, exhibit #31. While the entire video footage is not available, there are some stills from the video that can be seen in Anna Smolak's article '*People of No Consequence* by Aslan Gaisumov' (October 2016) at Mezosfera.org: available at https://bityl.co/AvAd

who have to bear the weight of this silence, which combines both a deep sense of personal loss, of homes lost in enforced resettlement, but also of memory and grief continuing to simmer in silence with undercurrents of anger. Deeply moving in its starkness and silence, the performance works against the grain of public mourning as commemorated in state archives through the corporeality of people assembled in a room—all of them survivors of mass displacement. Underlying the grief of this collective silence, there is a protest for lives lost. The people may remain unnamed but they assert themselves individually through their physical presence. Therein lies the political power and poignance of the work.

Spectacle

American artist Taryn Simon's monumental performance-installation on professional mourning, An *Occupation of Loss* (2016), involved professional mourners from over thirty different countries—Albania, Burkina Faso, Cambodia, Kyrgyzstan, Russia and Venezuela, among others.[60] The first iteration of this spectacular work was in New York during which Simon collaborated with Japanese architect Shohei Shigematsu, who designed 'eleven monolithic concrete cylinders'—'48-foot-tall, silo-like towers'

---

60 An *Occupation of Loss* was performed at the Park Avenue Armory, New York, 13–25 September 2016, and in Islington, London, 17–28 April 2018. It has been massively documented on a double album of live recordings from the London performance as well as studio recordings of each lament, Vinyl Factory, London, 2019. A video excerpt of the documentation of the London production (10 June 2020), directed by Boris Benjamin Bertram, can be seen at https://ytube.io/3PtM. There are at least two video presentations of Taryn Simon at Park Avenue Armory, New York—'Taryn Simon's An *Occupation of Loss*' (13 September 2016), available at https://ytube.io/3PtN; and 'Taryn Simon: Research on "An Occupation of Loss"' (23 September 2016), available at https://ytube.io/3PtO.

positioned in a semi-circle.⁶¹ Each of the towers had a long ramp leading into a doorway of small, bunker-like rooms, in which—either individually or in groups of two or three—the professional mourners sang, chanted, wept and played instruments like cymbals and drums, dressed in their 'native' outfits. Inevitably, these multi-vocal sonic resonances and echoes had a powerful sensory and auditory effect on the New York audience, even as one needs to keep in mind that almost all the professional mourners in Simon's installation represented non-Western lamentation traditions.

The title of the piece, An Occupation of Loss, is itself telling of the contradictions that Simon as a conceptual artist attempted to inscribe in the overall dramaturgy and conception of the work. At one level, the word 'occupation' refers to 'profession', in terms of what mourners actually *do* for their livelihood. However, 'occupation' also has more sinister echoes in the wider political domain, as in the Occupation of the West Bank by Israeli forces and other occupations in the war zones of the world. In this sense, there is something coercive about the word, which inevitably calls into play the dynamics of appropriation: An Occupation of Loss could also be read as An Appropriation of Loss.

Significantly, the militarist echoes of 'occupation' were inevitably enhanced by the actual building which housed Simon's installation in New York—the Park Avenue Armory, built in 1880 as a military facility with its 'soaring column-free 55,000-square-foot' Drill Hall resembling the Grand Central Depot and

---

61 All material relating to the description of Simon's installation at an architectural level and in relation to its multiple components is drawn from Lizzie Crocker, 'How Taryn Simon Created a Global Language of Grief', *Daily Beast*, 13 April 2017: available at https://bityl.co/AvAp. Simon's installation is also discussed in Cools, *Performing Mourning*, pp. 129–31. Vivid images of the installation's scenography can be seen in the video documentations mentioned in n. 60, which also provide conceptual insights into Simon's critical practice.

other massive train sheds.[62] Today, however, this space has been converted into a site for cutting-edge, spectacular artistic events operating at a scale that far surpasses what could be produced in a 'regular' theatre or museum or exhibition space. Not surprisingly, *An Occupation of Loss* was described by at least one of its appreciative critics as a 'paranormal or post-apocalyptic kingdom'[63]—a description that camouflaged the building's more mundane historical associations with a military space and storehouse of weapons.

The other keyword in the title is 'loss', which plays on both 'the loss of meaning and the meaning of loss'.[64] In this regard, Simon almost flaunted the fact that there was no specific object of loss around which the performances of the professional mourners were configured in their individual spaces. Instead, she went out of her way to *decontextualize* the different performances which were divested of any historical or conceptual references. It is possible to justify this choice at a purely aesthetic level in terms of facilitating a purely sensory experience of the sounds and cries of different lamentations. But it becomes more problematic to relate this 'experience' to the concept of 'agency' that Simon specifically links to the individual mourners. For Simon, the agency of the performers was to be traced in the way they appeared to guide the overall performance of grief *on their own terms* without the help of 'context or language'.[65] I would question this assumption not least

---

62 More details on the history of the building of the Park Avenue Armory can be read at https://www.armoryonpark.org/about_us/history

63 Crocker, 'How Taryn Simon Created a Global Language of Grief'.

64 Crocker, 'How Taryn Simon Created a Global Language of Grief'.

65 Crocker, 'How Taryn Simon Created a Global Language of Grief'. Crocker makes the point that '[Simon] was also interested in having the mourners in a space without context or language, where professional mourners could "claim agency and perform and guide and shape that abstract space".' Contrary to

because Simon failed to problematize the obvious fact—that the 'agency' of the performance had been obviously framed by *her* design, temporality, space and intention as an artist.

Drawing on Homi Bhabha's construct of the 'Third Space' from the 1990s, Simon also emphasized how the space of her installation intended to explore the interstices between what is real and what is imagined, a space that could collapse 'reality' and 'fiction' into a blurred entity.[66] Other oppositions she attempted to blur included the 'scripted' and the 'authentic', 'day' and 'night', the 'living' and the 'dead', 'scale' and 'invisibility', the 'singular voice' and 'cacophony', the 'invisible' and the 'visible'.[67] More than simply as a subjective expression of an idea or emotion, Simon justified her overall concept as operating at the level of translation between what is 'felt' at an authentic and existential level and how it is 'structured' at the level of abstraction. We have already discussed how individual performers like Ader and Kjartansson have dealt with abstracting grief in their solo performances. Simon's project, I would argue, was significantly different—she was not just exploring her grief; she was using over thirty professional mourners from diverse cultures to create a global spectacle of grief. What conceptual contribution, if any, could these mourners

---

Crocker's assumptions that the mourners were not using 'language', one should point out that they were, even as these languages may have been chanted or sung; the reality is that this babel of *languages* in at least 30 mother-tongues operated at a non-verbal level in the absence of any translation during the course of the performance.

66 In *The Location of Culture* (London and New York: Routledge, 1994), Homi K. Bhabha links the 'Third Space' to the 'in-between', the 'interstitial' and the 'hybrid' in order to ignite a process that 'gives rise to something different, something new and unrecognisable, a new area of negotiation of meaning and representation' (p. 211).

67 These oppositional categories are drawn from the video presentation of 'Taryn Simon: Research on "An Occupation of Loss"'.

have made in relation to Simon's larger treatment of abstraction? And what did they feel about performing their traditional laments, without any specific death or loss to mourn?

The crucial question that needs to be asked is: For whom was this spectacle of grief being performed? Clearly, for global, New York–based art consumers, who could bring to this spectacle whatever they wanted at an affective, emotional or aesthetic level. There is no consideration in Simon's larger conceptual scheme of how the 'mourners' themselves could have felt about being slotted into this performance, apart from the fact that they were duly paid for their services. Much more could be said about Simon's installation, not just in the context of its New York staging but also in relation to its metamorphosis in London in 2018 in a different avatar. Here, from the heights of Shigematsu's monumental towers, the new scenography of The Occupation of Loss evoked a 'descent into the underworld', as it was staged in the underground recesses of an abandoned car park.[68] Yet another spectacle, but with a different tonality and register.

Much has been made of the fact that at the end of the performance, both in New York and in London, all the visitors were presented with a text that included historical and anthropological material on the different traditions of 'professional mourning' represented in An Occupation of Loss.[69] More provocatively, this booklet also included all the paperwork that had to be submitted

---

[68] A different atmosphere was created for Simon's 'An Occupation of Loss' in London, where critic Adrian Searle of The Guardian (18 April 2018), described the space as 'both ancient and modern, a Piranesian vault, a sunken coliseum' with 'the feel of a sci-fi fantasy set, or some chapel of an unknown faith driven deep into the Earth'. See 'Taryn Simon: An Occupation of Loss review—Transfixing Cacophony from a Secret Underworld': available at https://bityl.co/AvAy

[69] Searle, 'Taryn Simon: An Occupation of Loss review'.

by Simon and the organizers of the event in order to obtain visas for the overseas participants. This is where the 'political' dimension of Simon's installation was most explicitly emphasized, not least by the artist herself, who seemed to belabour the point that the performances of professional mourners were made possible only through her difficult negotiations with the US and UK Departments of Immigration. Working as a surrogate visa agent was part of her 'cultural work' as an artist and an additional perspective on the larger politics of engaging with global cultural exchange.

Shifting the focus away from Simon, a more serious investigation of *The Occupation of Loss* in the larger context of the politics of mourning would necessitate a focus on the professional mourners as performers. What was *their* assessment of singing their mourning songs for six days a week to strangers who knew nothing about their language or culture or history? Could 'performing mourning' in these artistic circumstances have made any sense to the mourners? Or did they just 'turn on' their performances mechanically, as professional mourners are known to do? Far too many questions remain unanswered in the orchestration of this installation, which strikes me as being so master-minded that we never once get to sense a possible 'loss' that the *mourners* might have felt in Simon's 'occupation' of their time, energy and performative talents. Perhaps another installation is in order where the mourners could be invited not just to sing and chant and grieve, but also to speak and debate and argue about their incorporation within a First World global-art economy.

RUDALI: MOURNING AS SURVIVAL

I would now like to turn to the Indian context of representing the act of 'professional mourning' through an examination of Mahasweta Devi's radical short story *Rudali*.[70] The contrast with *An Occupation of Loss* could not be more emphatic, but it highlights a critical dimension in the larger context of mourning that has not figured in the discussion so far—not so much the aesthetics of mourning but the very real struggle for livelihood by professional mourners from the subaltern sectors of society. Apart from Devi's text of *Rudali* (in Bengali), I will also reflect, marginally, on a theatre production of the narrative in Hindi, which was powerfully adapted by director Usha Ganguli and staged in Calcutta in 1992. Unlike the avant-garde visual treatment of 'professional mourning' in Taryn Simon's installation, *Rudali* has to be seen in the context of popular theatre in a social-realist mode which ran for over a hundred performances for audiences in Indian cities and in the rural areas as well.

The word *rudali* refers to 'female weepers' or 'weeping women', generally from lower-caste backgrounds, who are hired to sing for funeral ceremonies in the households of upper-caste landlords and farmers. While they are generally identified as living in the western state of Rajasthan in India, although in decreasing numbers, Mahasweta Devi situates the phenomenon of the *rudali* in the rural borderlands of the eastern states of West Bengal and

---

70 Mahasweta Devi, *Rudali: From Fiction to Performance* (Anjum Katyal trans. and introd.) (Calcutta: Seagull Books, 2007[1997]). While I will be drawing closely on Katyal's translation for my analysis of the short story, I will not be providing an analysis of the playscript, focusing on the production of *Rudali* through a conversation with its director Usha Ganguli. Nor do I deal with the film adaptation of *Rudali* by Kalpana Lajmi in 1993, which departed quite significantly from the original story.

Bihar, focusing on the most destitute and landless of labourers from the 'untouchable' communities.

Strikingly, at no point in the story does Devi actually quote from any song belonging to the rudali tradition—and, in this sense, she is not drawing on the 'authentic' lamentation songs of the professional mourners, as exemplified in Simon's *An Occupation of Loss*. Neither is Devi's dramaturgy linked to any anthropological fieldwork or ethnography of grief as evident in Cools' account of the *moirologhia*, songs of lamentation performed during funereal wakes in Greece by semi-professional women mourners, who lament the dead person and carry on conversations with him or her.[71] Cools has observed closely the ways in which these women can be said to ventriloquize the voices of the dead in 'antiphonic, dialogic structures', where the singing is interspersed with a non-verbal score alternating between 'sobbing and discourse, between language and non-language'.[72] There is no such attention to the vocal details of traditional mourning practices in Devi's reading of the professional practices of the rudali, which are represented in a more generalized and robust register. In this sense, Devi makes no attempt to highlight grief, as evoked, for instance, in *An Occupation of Loss* through the sounds, cries, cadences, pitches and rhythms of songs sung and chanted by 'real' professional mourners. Instead of songs, what Devi focuses on are the chants and rhythmic actions and gestures of the *rudalis*, less in a ritualistic context of 'authentic' mourning and more in the framework of an improvised set of performative tactics for the larger politics of economic survival.

Keeping the motif of 'survival' in mind, my primary focus on *Rudali* can be linked to my earlier discussion of the internal

---

71 Cools, *Performing Mourning*, pp. 37–47.

72 Cools, *Performing Mourning*, p. 41.

migrant worker Rampukar Pandit, whose predicament on losing his infant son compelled him to acknowledge how the pain of his suffering was enhanced by the fact that he had no money or job. It is the task of feeding his family in a state of acute poverty that heightens Pandit's pain of losing his son. Even as there is no pandemic represented in the social background of *Rudali* but just the relentless grind of poverty and hunger that continues on a daily basis, the primary difference with Pandit's predicament has to do with the fact that while he cries on hearing that his son has died, the central character of Sanichari in *Rudali* cannot cry—she does not cry and will not cry even as she faces any number of deaths in her family. Grief is a 'luxury' for Sanichari; what matters is survival.

Through the sheer force of her words, Devi has the capacity to consolidate the tragedies of everyday life in a couple of sentences, calling attention to any number of caste-related cruelties and injustices in the representation of suffering and death. So, on the opening page of the story, we are told: 'When her mother-in-law died, Sanichari didn't cry' (p. 71). Her husband and brother-in-law are in prison, framed on false charges of theft by the feudal landowner. In a matter-of-fact, third-person narrative, Devi creates an entire scenario of the social pressures of death and mourning faced by untouchable communities:

> Sanichari and her sister-in-law together lowered the old woman on to the ground. If the rites weren't carried out before the night was over, they would have to bear the costs of the repentance rites for keeping the corpse in the house overnight. And there wasn't even a cupful of grain in the house! So Sanichari was forced to go from neighbour to neighbour in the pouring rain. Dragging the neighbours home with her, and handling all the arrangements for

the cremation, she was so busy that there was no time to cry (p. 72).

From this pithy description, it becomes clear that a 'delayed funeral' could be a source of punishment for Sanichari—the neighbours have to be 'dragged' into participating in the rituals, so that she can avoid paying a penalty for violating the decorum of prescribed funeral rites.

Sanichari is less lucky in saving on money when her husband dies after drinking contaminated milk offered to a Shiva idol at a village fair. He dies of cholera. Here in a fleeting reference to colonial rule—the British administration is still in power—we are made to see how the government officials 'drag' the contaminated to hospital tents. Sanichari and her son Budhua wait outside the barbed wire surrounding the tents. Once again, Devi wastes no time in getting to the bare facts of the tragedy: 'The government officers didn't give her any time to shed tears. They burned the corpses quickly. They dragged Sanichari and Budhua off for a vaccination against the disease. The pain of the injection made them howl' (pp. 73–4).

Almost like a premonition of our own times, when vaccination can become a source of terror for those who are coerced into taking a shot, Devi provides a glimpse of the medicalization of the body to which I had referred in the first chapter. There I had called attention to the Bombay plague of 1896 when the rules and regulations of the colonial medical system were imposed on the population.

Along with the colonial machinery, which makes its appearance only once in Devi's story, there is a ceaseless reminder of the oppressive mechanisms of religious rituals. Far from consoling people after their loved ones die, the tyranny of religion only succeeds in rendering destitute people bankrupt: the burden of ritualizing grief only leads to onerous debts and, on occasion, a submission to bonded labour. This is Sanichari's lot because she has to pay for two sets of rituals—one at the site of the fair where her husband died, and another at home in her village, where the local priest castigates her for following the rituals of another Brahmin priest who is ignorant of the local customs.

And so, life goes on for Sanichari. Or, as Devi puts it in a harsher ironic register, 'Time passes on an empty stomach' (p. 75).

Later in the story, in what may be seen as a happy turn of events, Sanichari meets up with an old childhood friend, Bikhni, and the two middle-aged women set up home together. On the pragmatic advice of a shrewd man in the community, they are introduced to the idea of professional mourning. At first Sanichari doubts her credentials: 'Cry? Me? Don't you know? I can't shed tears. These two eyes of mine are scorched?' (p. 90). Ultimately convinced that the *randis* (prostitutes) discarded by the landown-ers don't make 'convincing rudalis', Sanichari and Bikhni enter the trade for their livelihood. They already have the appropriate cos-tume for the job, because they wear black in everyday life. So, appropriately attired, they wail so loudly at the funeral that they are duly fed by their upper-caste oppressors with all the obligatory offerings of food; they are also gifted cloth, and most of all, money.

Sanichari proves to be a pragmatic businesswoman, as she lays down the terms of 'performing mourning':

> Just for wailing, one kind of rate. Wailing and rolling on the ground, five rupees one sikka (quarter of a rupee). Wailing, rolling on the ground and beating one's chest, five rupees two sikkas. Wailing and beating one's breast, accompanying the corpse to the cremation ground, rolling around on the ground there—for that the charge is six rupees (pp. 96–7).

Business prospers and the rates go up, and the landlords begin to vie with one another to get the two women to mourn their dead, almost like a 'war of prestige'. Some of them even reject the possibility of medication while falling ill in order to imagine grand funerals after their imminent deaths. It is not lost on either of the women that these benefactors are also their exploiters, but who are themselves exploited by their surrender to ritual. Long live feudal ignorance and upper-caste stupidity.

Following the one jolt in the story when Bikhni dies suddenly, for which there is no preparation, Sanichari continues to survive, rallying the prostitutes in her area, including her former daughter-in-law, to wail in unison at funerals. In a sense, she becomes the chief organizer of mourning. In the closing lines of the story, we learn how as the 'rotting flesh' of the landlord's corpse is stinking, the rudalis are wailing and banging their heads (thereby ensuring that they will be paid double). In this tumult of histrionic lamentation, one of the prostitutes looks up with dry eyes and winks at the nephew of the bereaved family, before returning to wail in the chorus of rudalis. This is an earthy and caustic reminder that the sex trade does not have to stop with mourning, but can be a source of titillation as a side-business, contributing to the livelihood of women.

The contrast with Simon's An Occupation of Loss could not be more stark. For Devi, it is not the 'authenticity' or ritual gravity of professional mourning that is of concern; what matters is a simulation of grief as a mode of livelihood. What matters is not the psychophysical histrionics of mourning, supplemented by cries and wails and nonverbal sounds, but the social context that illuminates how rituals of mourning can be exploitative for the poor. To subvert the ritualistic framework is the only means of survival. There is no sentimentality or sense of loss in this enactment of subversion. In contrast, Simon's installation goes out of its way to 'respect' the individual autonomy of the mourners from different cultures, even as one could question how this 'autonomy' is framed in the first place. Another conclusion that could be drawn from a juxtaposition of these two works of arts is that when Simon focuses on the economy of the professional mourners, she calls attention to her efforts in getting them to travel from their faraway locations to New York and London. There is no elaboration as such on how much the professional mourners in her installation were paid. On the other hand, the professional mourners in Devi's story need no professional mediation as they bargain on their own terms for what their mourning is worth, not just in terms of religious sublimation or soothing the souls of the grieved but also in terms of hard cash.

* * *

Let me now shift the focus from fiction to theatre. In a bold and vibrant production, cast in the idiom of social realism, with strongly realized characters and robust stage action, including fights and heartfelt 'wailing' sessions bordering on farce, accompanied by breast beating and the flailing of hands, Usha Ganguly's *Rudali* was a virtuoso, yet very close rendition of Devi's story. The one significant point of departure in the play text was to be found in its representation of Bikhni's death. While Bikhni dies off-stage, Sanichari (played by Usha Ganguly) responds to it at first in a matter-of-fact way, but later, when she is left alone, she breaks down before collecting herself. Her tears seems like a perfectly 'natural' way of expressing the grief of losing a dearly beloved sister-friend. But this is totally counter to what Mahasweta Devi has in mind:

What did she feel? Grief? No, not grief, fear. Her husband had died, her son had died, her grandson had left, her daughter-in-law had run away—there had always been grief in her life. But she [had] never felt this devouring fear before. Bikhni's death affected her livelihood, her profession, that's why she's experiencing this fear. And why, after all? Because she's old. Amongst them, one works, if one can, till one's last breath. Ageing means growing old. Growing old means not being able to work. And that means death (p. 114).

This is as terse and unsentimental a reflection on what it means to age and die, for which there is no time to mourn, except, of course, if one is a rudali and can earn a livelihood through mourning until one's dying breath.

The emotional intensity and subversive power of Devi's dark humour are often lost in translation. Suffice it to say that the ironic vision of the story is concretized through a particular grammar whose syntax is based on enjambments and sharp juxtapositions of third-person commentary and first-person utterance, spliced with snatches of dialogue incorporating words not normally found in the Bengali vocabulary. Instead, the characters use the patois of everyday life among the most destitute classes. In this assemblage of dialects and local idioms, Devi occasionally inserts official categories in English—for instance, *gormen* (for government) and *pishiden* (for president)—demonstrating the savage humour with which she decolonizes the Bengali language. More irreverently, she intersperses the images of gods and goddesses with calendar art and matinee idols from popular cinema to create a subaltern imaginary for the worldview of her illiterate protagonists.

Far from lapsing into naturalism, Devi employs what could be described as an 'epic' language—not the epic of the Sanskrit renderings of the Mahabharata but a Mahabharata of the down-trodden, an *itihasa* (history) of everyday struggle and survival. Inevitably, although in a different register and cultural context, one is reminded of Brecht and his ways of 'interrupting' language and inserting 'quotes' to break the flow of words. Not surprisingly, given her predilection for epic narratives, Usha Ganguli is also known for her production of *Himmat Mai*, her adaptation in Hindi of *Mother Courage*, in which she played the title role.

What struck me most about this adaptation was the way in which Mother Courage's legendary wagon, on which she travels and crosses borders, buying and selling different commodities, while her children die during the war, took on a distinctly new avatar in the Hindi adaptation as a *thelagari*. This is a cart made out of long bamboo poles positioned on wheels, which is either dragged in front by a labourer or pushed from behind by another, or, in some cases, dragged and pushed at the same time to give it momentum. The thelagari continues to be used in Indian cities for transporting large sacks of grain or other heavy merchandise. So arduous is the labour that goes into this transportation that the carriers could be described with no exaggeration as 'beasts of burden'.

At a preview of *Himmat Mai*, I shared with Usha how moved I was by the use of the thelagari. Like the wagon in *Mother Courage*, it became a character in its own right, with each functional detail of the cart painstakingly worked out, as it dominated the stage with an elemental force. Unlike the wagon, however, which is an anachronism in Western countries today, most likely to be seen in a country fair or a performative re-enactment of colonial history from an earlier pre-industrial period, the thelagari continues to be a recognizable part of street life in most parts of India, particularly in working-class districts and areas dominated by wholesale markets.

While talking to Usha, I found myself remembering a particularly painful sight of a dead bovine strapped to a thelagari with a
rope. As the thelagari seemed to glide past the window of the taxi
in which I was seated, I could see in a split second the eyes of the
labourer pushing the bamboo cart—eyes that were so stricken
with grief that they appeared to be sunken, hollow, almost dead.
In that instant, I realized that the man was in all probability taking
the dead animal to the abattoir for its skin to be stripped from its
skeletal frame and sold along with its flesh. For the labouring class,
there is always some money to be made from death, even if the
death is painful and experienced with stoic endurance.

It may seem odd that I should share such a personal moment
from a Calcutta street scene with Usha but it was sparked by the
thelagari, which had played such a vital role in her rendering of a
distinctly Indian Mother Courage (Himmat Mai). Usha understood what I was attempting to point out—the extremity to which
the struggle for survival can be sustained for which there is no
time to cry. As, indeed, Sanichari has no need to cry: she cannot
cry. But she lives, just as Mother Courage survives, avoiding
the obligatory anguish of a mother on hearing about her son's
death, by substituting her cry for a 'silent scream'. Brecht leaves us
to ponder this moment through our involuntary tears, as I find
myself strangely affected on reminding myself that my theatre
friend Usha has passed on. Is what I am writing a way of mourning
for her?

MAYA KRISHNA RAO, PERFORMING *WALK* AT JANTAR MANTAR, NEW DELHI, 22 JANUARY 2013.

WALK: MOURNING AS RESISTANCE

Is one to assume that economic realities and poverty obliterate the possibility of mourning? Or would it be more appropriate to think of other subterranean ways in which mourning does manifest itself? Can mourning go underground? Can it be temporarily suspended? Or, more precisely, can it be 'transformed', to use a keyword by Judith Butler, in her attempt to work against a 'privatizing' understanding of grief and to see how the transformed state of grief can mobilize 'a sense of political community'?[73]

It is in response to this last possibility that I offer these reflections on Maya Krishna Rao's explosive performance of *Walk*, which was improvised in direct response to the brutal rape and torture of Jyoti Singh in a moving bus in New Delhi on 16 December 2012. Singh's rape galvanized the Indian public, normally immune to the daily assault on women in public spaces, and she became an iconic figure at a national level. Under the guise of protecting her 'privacy', she was first identified under the pseudonym 'Nirbhaya' [Fearless], until it was her mother, perhaps the woman with the deepest right to grieve at a personal level, who insisted that her daughter should be identified by her own name: Jyoti Singh.

It could be argued that the dead do not need pseudonyms, even as this may be the case for how some 'terrorists' get marked, if they are mourned at all, following their deaths. It is an insufficiently acknowledged fact that the dead bodies of terrorists are rarely claimed after a terror attack in order to be buried or cremated; such attempts by civilians to claim the bodies could be condemned as 'anti-national'. Perhaps, the unclaimed bodies of the most criminalized elements in society would fall under the

---

73 Butler, *Precarious Life*, p. 22.

category of the 'ungrievable', as Butler has theorized so powerfully. Today, the 'ungrievable' constitutes a large category of an
increasing number of 'undocumented' people, including migrants,
minorities and refugees across the world, people often assumed
not to be 'human'. Even more brutally, they may not be considered
to 'exist' at all.

> They [the ungrievable] cannot be mourned because they
> are always already lost or, rather, never 'were', and they
> must be killed, since they seem to live on, stubbornly, in
> this state of deadness. [. . .] The derealization of the 'Other'
> means that it is neither alive nor dead, but interminably
> spectral.[74]

Arguably, there was nothing 'spectral' about Jyoti Singh's
condition—it was only too 'real', if not palpable. She was emi-
nently 'grievable', but the question is: How is she to be mourned?
How can the grief following her death which got consolidated in
public demonstrations on the streets of New Delhi and other
Indian cities be rendered through performance? The challenge of
any such performance, to my mind, is to ensure that it does not
perpetuate the exploitation of Jyoti Singh's mutilated body and the
political hypocrisy surrounding it. In this context, I do believe
that Rao's *Walk* is an exemplary performance in the way it mobi-
lizes public grief into collective political rage and action.

While the production has gone through any number of iterations, with each performance being radically altered according to
the performative circumstances and the spatial and temporal
demands of each performance, what I am addressing here are its
very first iterations, drawing on numerous video recordings of the
performance and a working script that Maya (as I know her) has

---

74 Butler, *Precarious Life*, pp. 33–4.

shared with me. The 'premiere', if you will, of this assertively agit-prop piece of activist theatre was first performed on the campus of Jawaharlal Nehru University (JNU) in New Delhi a few days after the death of Jyoti Singh, on the request of students protesting the rape. Over the years, subsequent performances of *Walk* have come to resemble a more structured form of 'applied theatre' where Rao's focus is less on agit-prop politics and more on the debates and negotiations around 'consensus' in sexual matters.

The first thing to note about the script of *Walk* is that it does not mention Jyoti Singh at all. There is no explicit homage paid to her as a martyr or as a victim; still less are there any references to the brutal circumstance of her death and details of torture. Such a literal representation of violence, which is often found in 'documentary theatre', is anathema to Maya at both aesthetic and ethical levels. More to the point of this argument, such a representation has no specific relevance to what Maya chooses to highlight in her performance, which can be communicated in one word: 'Walk'. Thus the play is not so much a lament for a dead woman, whose spirit may be said to animate the performance, as it is an exhortation to all the women in the audience to claim the right to 'walk'.

This is the opening word of the text as Maya lunges forwards on the platform with a thrust of her arm upwards and shouts, 'WALK.' In that first beat, there is, almost inevitably, a sense of jubilation in the audience, particularly when the play is staged outdoors in activist sites and forums. It is almost as if the audience is waiting to hear this word to transform their grief and confusion and fear into some form of collective defiance.

Shrewdly, Maya intersperses her text with a play of numbers:

One ... two ... one step at a time
Not 5, 6, 7, not 8
... at 12 midnight, [*here her voice peaks in a crescendo*]

I want to walk the streets of Delhi . . . my city
Sit on a bus, cross the road
Lie in the park, not afraid of the dark[75]

All these words are spoken in sync with a catchy musical background downloaded from a YouTube music channel that continues relentlessly with an insistent rhythm. To this sound-track, the tone of the performance is anything but solemn or merely declamatory but more like a cross between hip hop, rap and improv.

The numbers inscribed in the text are occasionally spliced with factual evidence. As, for instance:

In 2012 in Delhi there were 754 cases registered [against rape]
Convictions? Not 5 . . . not 4 . . . not 3
They say, just 1, *matr* [only] 1

Along with numbers, Maya also splices short phrases in Hindi into the predominantly English text, which serve as enjambments and punctuation points. As she creates a sense of threat in evoking the passing of time, she falls back on an incremental use of numbers in Hindi: *paune do, sava teen, sade char* (a quarter to two, a quarter past three, half past four).

Against the numbers and facts, all rendered in the third person, Maya falls back on the personal pronoun 'I' to pronounce her

---

75 I am grateful to Maya Krishna Rao for sharing the script which, for all the improvisatory quality of her numerous performances of *Walk*, remains a strong point of reference. I will quote directly from the script, which has not yet been published. Since there is no pagination, I will not be indicating any page numbers in my text. Among the numerous video documentations of the performance, I would recommend https://ytube.io/3RPj, Jantar Mantar, New Delhi, 22 February 2013, and https://ytube.io/3RPk, Jawaharlal Nehru University, 11 July 2020.

most emphatic declaration of solidarity—explicitly with the
women in the audience, even as men can be seen cheering along:

> I know when to say yes
> I've learnt when to say no
> Yes, I'll talk to you don't talk to him
> Don't give him a job, don't vote for him
> I'll walk with you . . .

For an enactment by a solo woman performer in the contemporary Indian public sphere, where women are ceaselessly
harassed, stalked, touched, molested, stared at and raped, this
assertion of intimacy—'Don't walk with him, I'll walk with
you'—is at once audacious and bold. Without sexualizing the
remark, there *is* a sexual charge to the words not least because
Maya's voice and presence are often described as 'male' by her vast
body of fans from the LGBTQIA+ community. This persona could,
at one level, be attributed to the fact that, as a performer who has
received her basic training in Kathakali, she has always been
drawn to 'male' roles, notably Ravana, the most compelling of male
daemonic figures in Indian mythology.[76]

But, in *Walk*, what we see on stage is not Ravana but a woman
in her sixties with a long mane of white hair, in a cotton sari
wrapped around her in a matter-of-fact way, declaiming to the
audience what appears to be a manifesto:

> A man who looks not at a woman right
> A man who sits not with a woman right

---

[76] In my essay 'Ravana as Dissident Artist', in Paula Richman and Rustom
Bharucha (eds), *Performing the Ramayana Tradition: Enactments, Interpreta-
tions, and Arguments* (New York: Oxford University Press, 2021), pp. 142–57,
I provide an annotation of Rao's highly deconstructive reading of Ravana in
Ravanama. This 'performance text' is more fragmented and allusive than *Walk*.

A man who treats not a woman right
A man who touches not a woman right
A man who talks not to a woman right
Who cares not for a woman right
Who cares not for another man, a boy right
A man who respects not his wife right

Such a man needs to be shunned but not without the hope that there will be re-inventions of fathers, in addition to new incarnations of sons, daughters and mothers: the father will bring up his daughter in the same way that he brings up his son; the son will know what it is to be a daughter; the daughter will be more and more herself; and the mother will stand up to a *mama* (maternal uncle) and *chacha* (paternal uncle), who are unable to differentiate between love and aggression. In these fervent pleas—'Give me a father, give me a son, give me a daughter, give me a mother', a new sociality is being envisioned, which is based not just on a critique of patriarchy but also on an unsettling of the existing kinship system.

In an odd way—and the reference may seem totally out of context—one is reminded of Antigone here. At one level, unlike Antigone who has been ordered not to bury her brother Polyneices by the edict of the State, the unnamed woman being played by Maya in *Walk* is not being denied the right to grieve. Her sister, Jyoti Singh, may have died in brutal circumstances, but far from prohibiting her funerary rites and cremation, the state has gone out of its way to show how much it 'cares' for its daughter-citizens. While there is no reason to believe in its patriarchal care, there is no direct prohibition against the right to mourn, unlike in today's India whose citizens are being warned, however implicitly, against displaying their vulnerability. (Keep in mind the solicitor general's remark, 'Let's try and not be a cry baby.') At a legal level, the law courts even proved to be proactive in the case of Jyoti Singh's rape: four of her rapists were sentenced to death; another (the alleged ringleader) died by suicide in prison; and the youngest (and allegedly the most ruthless) received a reprieve on account of his age. Countering the usual dismal record of 'justice delayed' as 'justice denied', the state courts administered their task with efficiency.

This does not mean that one can ignore the horrifying evidence. *Walk* asserts in its opening lines that, in 2012, there were 754 registrations of rape of which only one received a conviction. The Law remains anti-woman in its massive indifference to the daily crimes of violence against women. In order to fight it, one has no option but to extend the struggle not merely by opposing the agencies of the State, the Law and Police, but—this is the crucial point—by envisioning a new sociality which necessitates a dismantling of the existing kinship system, as Maya posits in the text of her performative manifesto.

It is in this articulation of sociality and kinship that I find some ground of similarity with Butler's argument that, '[I]n acting, as one who has no right to act, [Antigone] upsets the vocabulary of kinship that is a precondition of the human, implicitly raising the question for us of what those preconditions really must be.' Butler goes on to argue a more complex point that, 'If kinship is the precondition of the human, then Antigone is the occasion for a new field of the human, [. . .] the one that happens when the less than human speaks as human, when gender is displaced, and kinship founders on its own found laws.'[77]

Walk does not go so far as to posit a new epistemology of the 'human', nor does it 'displace' gender, even as the text reasserts

---

77 Judith Butler, *Antigone's Claim: Kinship between Life and Death* (New York: Columbia University Press, 2000), p. 82.

new, unimagined rights for women, beginning with the most fundamental 'right to walk'—'walk' signifying all that is open to being free, driven by one's own agency, and with no internalization of patriarchal inhibitions. By embracing the word *azadi* (freedom)—most ardent of battle cries for all kinds of freedom, even as the state would like to restrict it (and thereby demonize it) by equating it with the right for self-determination in Kashmir—*Walk* builds to a thrilling coda where 'azadi' is repeated over and over again in a range of situations:

> Can I just walk?
> Can I just walk?
> Into a lift, free, out of a lift, free
> Into bed free, out of bed free
> Into a bus free, on the street free
>
> Sadak pe azadi (Free on the street)
> Lift mein azadi (Free in a lift)
> Bistar mein azadi (Free in bed)
> Office mein azadi (Free in the office)
> Decision mein azadi (Free to make decisions)
> Kapdon mein azadi (Freedom of clothes)
> Make-up ki azadi (. . . of make-up)

Walk makes one realize the multiple freedoms of the quotidian, for which no new laws are likely to be written. The only option is to take the struggle to the streets by holding *mashaals* (fire torches), thereby lighting up every lane, every one of 'the 22,000 unlit lanes in Delhi', as reported by the Delhi Police Commissioner. Once again, Maya shrewdly appropriates this official statistic into her text and juxtaposes the absence of electric lights with the presence of mashaals—one of the most potent symbols of protest that has been used in all kinds of subaltern and mass movements, leaving behind in the political unconscious deeply imprinted images of tongues of flame illuminating the darkness.

Not content to build the incremental registers of resistance through the image of the mashaal—this could have provided a nice 'revolutionary' climax to her piece—Maya once again cuts the promise of an insurgency of struggle with a more domestic and private illumination of marital rape:

> But it's not just the dark that I fear
> When I open the door to my home
> It's lit up
> I can see the man who does it
> Have known him, have trusted him,
> Have made my home, my children with him . . .
> It's the man I thought I knew . . .

Here again one is compelled to rethink the politics of kinship at the most intimate level of domesticity and marriage, because the man 'I thought I knew' is no different from other men the woman encounters in the home, in a restaurant, in the office, in a party, in a field, in a *jhopdi* (hut). Juxtaposing the public and the private through explicit and hidden forms of violence, Maya compels one to 'think'. This is probably one of the most moving moments in my experience of the performance as a spectator, when Maya stops dead in her tracks and raises her hands to her forehead, her body slightly bent, as she affirms the need to think. If *Walk* had been a performance only charged with activist fire, it would not have 'worked' as powerfully. But it is the alchemy with which the cry for action is balanced with other thoughts of fear, regret, inaction and habitual endurance that the 'mourning' for Jyoti Singh, while never explicitly stated or commemorated, is nonetheless the animating force of the performance.

'To grieve, and to make grief itself into a resource for politics,' as Butler puts it so succinctly, 'is not to be resigned to inaction.'[78] This statement is clearly demonstrated in the febrile, yet concentrated, dynamics of *Walk* and the tumultuous response of the audience to the cry for action on stage. There can be no resignation to 'inaction' at this point in time in India, even as there are new levels of intimidation and threat faced by political demonstrators of 'action', whether it involves the farmers' movement and the fight against the imposition of new citizenship laws.

However, to return to Butler's claim that grief as a resource for politics is not to be aligned with inaction, she does add an important caveat, as she envisions the mobilization of grief as 'the slow process by which we develop a point of identification with suffering itself.'[79] I am not sure that agit-prop performance can be expected to highlight the unravelling of grief as a slow process, given that by its very nature and structure it is more like a fast-paced series of exhortations and thoughts, packed into a concentrated period of time. This does not mean, of course, that there cannot be other forms of activist performance, which could explore a long duration of interventions in public spaces through silence and meditative actions, or site-specific vigils commemorating the dead.[80] The possibilities of performing mourning in other temporalities and modalities remain open for other kinds

---

78 Butler, *Precarious Life*, p. 30.

79 Butler, Precarious Life, p. 30.

80 A strong example of a long-term, site-specific protest vigil and call for action would be the movement around the Mothers of the Plaza de Mayo in Buenos Aires, Argentina, which has been in existence since 1977. Continuing to protest against the disappearance of those children and young adults who were targeted by military forces and right-wing death squads, the 'mothers' continue to protest and make their presence felt in the Plaza de Mayo with extraordinary resilience. See the Wikipedia entry on Mothers of the Plaza de Mayo for more information on the recent configurations of the movement.

of intervention, which does not rule out the pertinence and immediacy of *Walk*, which captured the tumultuous grief of the political
moment surrounding Jyoti Singh's death with an unprecedented
immediacy and call to action.

MOURNING: PERFORMED OR REAL?

As I come to the end of this chapter, I would like to offer an
unprecedented 'performance' of mourning in everyday life. It
was not performed within the framework of any identifiable theatrical genre but, rather, was created at a personal level by a non-
professional in the very thick of the pandemic. What makes this
'performance' so very special and rare is that it was a response to
the last moments of a patient dying from Covid-19 in the hermetic
confines of an ICU ward. The patient herself was a mute spectator
and listener as she listened to the 'performance' recorded on a
smartphone by her son who grieved for her. Since he could not be
physically present in the ICU, the performance was communicated
to the dying patient through the mediation of a female doctor who
held up the smartphone to her. As the performance unfolded, there
was an audience in the ICU ward, as other nurses gathered around
and watched the final scene. They were the silent spectators.[81]

At every conceivable level, as I see it, this 'performance' breaks
all the norms that one associates with a rehearsed performance on

---

81 I draw my information of this painful event from numerous newspaper
articles, notably two pieces in *The Indian Express*: see 'Son Sings "Tera
Mujhse Hai" on Last Call to Woman Dying of Covid-19, Heartbroken Netizens Say "This Shouldn't Happen to Anyone"', 14 May 2021: available at
https://bityl.co/AvyC; and 'Man, Who Sang for His Dying Mother, Sings Again
in Tribute; Video Leaves People Emotional', 19 May 2021: available at:
https://bityl.co/AvyF. The actual song as performed by Soham Chatterjee
in honour of his mother Sanghamitra Chatterjee can be seen at https://-
bityl.co/AvyG

a regular stage or performance setting. And, in this crucial sense, it is an exception to the absence of autobiographical solo performances in contemporary Indian theatre that I have emphasized earlier. Here, we encounter a totally unprecedented performance of everyday life (and, one could add, parting moments in death), where the script, the song and the singer are meshed together with a startling directness of communication. It is the most intensely 'personal' form of improvised theatre.

In most media reports, the man doing the performance was identified as 'the son' who is performing for 'his mother', in the ICU ward at Apollo Gleneagles Hospital, Calcutta. Later, with the son's permission, they were identified as Mrs Sanghamitra Chatterjee and Soham Chatterjee. From the earliest reports, the 'stage-manager' of the performance was named—critical-care doctor Dipshikha Ghosh, who took on the role of the 'grief counsellor' or 'comforter' during the pandemic. She had played this role on previous occasions as she had attempted to connect terminally ill patients with their loved ones via video calls. Since the relatives could not enter the ICU and the dying patients were incarcerated in their beds, technology (via a smartphone) became the only means to convey the final goodbyes.

From a report published in *The Times of India* on 14 May 2021,[82] we learn how Dr Ghosh mediated between the son and the dying mother in her usual manner, combining professional discretion and emotional control as far as possible. But this time round, according to a message tweeted by Dr Ghosh and circulated widely in the public domain, there was a difference in the message communicated by the son to his mother, insofar as he began to sing a popular Hindi film song, *'Tera mujhse hai pehle ka naata koi'*

---

82 See Subhro Niyogi, 'Son Sings to Dying Mother: "Tera mujhse hai pehle ka naata koi . . ."', *The Times of India*, 14 May 2021: available at https://bityl.co/AvyJ

('We probably knew each other before this life') to his mother, a song they both loved. Drawn from an emotionally charged 1970s film titled *Aa gale lag jaa* (Come, embrace me) where a couple are separated only to be reunited via their son, the song has the following heartfelt lyrics:

> Look, don't get lost now
> Don't ever get separated from me,
> We still stay united this time:
> This is a promise we make today.
> Whether you know it or not.
> Whether you believe it or not.[83]

It is, indeed, both poignant and strange how the words of a song from a blatantly melodramatic film, whose drama is played out assertively with all the usual Hindi-film stereotypes, can get transferred to a 'real' death scene where a son sings to his dying mother. Following the video call, it seems that the mother passed away twelve hours later.

Curious to follow up on this intensely private performance, watched only by the nurses in the hospital ward, I tried to locate the song as it was sung in the hospital, only to realize that it was a 'live' call not meant to be disseminated. What does exist on YouTube, however, is another rendition of the song which is sung by the son with considerable composure and controlled grief. In the theoretical language of performance studies, this repetition of the performance can be regarded as an example of 'restored behaviour', a 'twice-behaved' behaviour that that has been 'rehearsed' on the basis of a pre-existing script and set of

---

83 The translation of the song is available at https://bityl.co/AvyM. It is composed by the legendary composer R. D. Burman and sung by the incomparable Kishore Kumar and Poornima, with lyrics by Sahir Ludhianvi.

performance codes.[84] While listening to the man sing, I was struck by the fact that he was hitting all the right notes even as an unprofessional singer. After singing, he paused and then shared a few words (in English), saying that his mother's death was inevitable, an act of destiny that could not be prevented, and he could only hope that she knew how much he loved her. At one level, these are platitudinous words to which we all tend to succumb at moments of loss, but there was a soothing quality to them—one could sense that the man was performing his mourning in a composed and self-regulated way. It was only too clear that he wanted to share his moment of grief with a wider public on the Internet.

This is not to assume that in coming to terms with grief that there is some kind of closure. All one can hope for is a process of mourning that gets integrated into everyday life, with highs and lows, moments of forgetting and remembrance, providing some psychological comfort and resilience to the persons affected by loss. On this hope, however tenuous, I will end this chapter.

---

84 'Restored behaviour' is one of the foundational concepts of 'performance' in Performance Studies and has received its earliest and most authoritative theorization by Richard Schechner, *Performative Circumstances: From the Avant-Garde to the Ramlila* (Calcutta: Seagull Books, 1983), pp. 164–237.

3.

Endings / Beginnings

What we call the beginning is often the end
And to make an end is to make a beginning.
The end is where we start from.

—T. S. Eliot, *Little Gidding*

During the worst days of the pandemic, when the usually cacophonous street outside my house was empty and silent, and so many people I knew were dying or had died, I often felt as though the world was coming to an end. Of course, this was a feeling: nothing more, nothing less. Calling our attention to the saying, 'There is no end,' philosopher Franco Berardi reminds us that it can be read in at least two different ways: as 'a source of endless despair', or as 'a source of endless hope'.[1] In both formulations, one could say that the definitive aura of 'the end' is better substituted by 'ending' or 'endings', insofar as 'the end' has not yet materialized, even though it may be looming ahead.

---

1 Franco Berardi, *AND: Phenomenology of the End* (Cambridge, MA: Semiotext(e) / Foreign Agents, 2015), p. 9.

If we read despair in the phrase 'there is no end', the suggestion is that the same set of problems may continue to plague us, the pandemic may never leave us; hence, 'there is no end'. However, one could also draw a more hopeful reading from the statement insofar as it calls attention to the mutations of everyday life, which are likely to continue in unpredictable ways. So, what can we do about it? For Berardi, both readings of 'there is no end' via 'endless despair' or 'endless hope' are 'on the wrong path'.[2] Instead, he substitutes the word 'end' with 'and', which is the single-word title of his book AND: *Phenomenology of the End* (2015). Why 'and'? Berardi calls our attention to the rhizome as a modality, theorized by Félix Guattari and Gilles Deleuze, in which 'endings and beginnings' are nullified:

> A rhizome has neither beginning nor end, but always a middle (milieu) between things, inter-being, *intermezzo*. The tree is filiation, but the rhizome is alliance, uniquely alliance. The tree imposes the verb 'to be', but the fabric of the rhizome is the conjunction, 'and . . . and . . . and . . .'. This conjunction carries enough force to shake and uproot the verb 'to be' [. . .] to establish a logic of the AND, overthrow ontology, do away with foundations, nullify endings and beginnings.[3]

Not in a position to 'overthrow ontology' or to 'do away with foundations', I would prefer in these reflections to substitute the logic of the AND with the more modest, yet tricky, modality of the *interstice*. This is not an attempt to let go of the notion of the 'end', or 'ends' or 'endings', but to insist that they cannot be entirely separated from diverse 'beginnings'.

---

2 Berardi, *AND*.

3 Berardi, *AND*. Berardi is quoting from *A Thousand Plateaus: Capitalism and Schizophrenia* (Minneapolis: University of Minnesota Press, 1987).

As I write these lines, there is an unexpected insight in the newspaper from the K-Pop boyband BTS, who recently danced and sang at the UN's New York headquarters. Endorsing the resilience of youth culture, which is not a 'lost culture' but 'the welcome generation' even in the age of the pandemic, vocalist Jungkook affirmed that the future should not be viewed with 'grim darkness'. Calling attention to people who continue to be 'concerned for the world and searching for the answers', Jungkook went on to say, *'we don't just talk about it like the ending is already written.'*[4] Bold words coming from the UN's Special Presidential Envoys for Future Generations and Culture, words which may need to be countered with the overwhelming scientific and ecological evidence of multiple endings of the world.

Perhaps, one needs to pause for a moment here to say that most of these 'endings' are still in the process of being articulated in the present continuous, with no definite 'end' in sight. Such a seemingly endless postponement of 'the end' may not fill us with the reckless hope of new generations to come, as affirmed by BTS. Instead, what comes to mind is 'dark hope', which is how Sanskritist and peace activist David Shulman has characterized the larger context of struggling for peace on the West Bank.[5] It is this hope that shadows my reflections on the interstice between endings and beginnings, which is the subject of this chapter.

---

4 *The Times of India*, 'BTS Deliver Powerful Speech on Climate Change, Importance of Covid Vaccine and Hope for the Future at UNGA; Say "Every Choice We Make Is the Beginning of Change"', 20 September 2021: available at https://bityl.co/BdLM (emphasis added).

5 David Shulman, *Dark Hope: Working for Peace in Israel and Palestine* (Chicago: University of Chicago Press, 2007).

EXIT

To ground the discussion of endings and beginnings, let us turn to the theatre, whose vocabulary often provides me with concrete illuminations of seemingly abstract thoughts. Among the many aspects of theatre as an institutionalized practice that are taken entirely for granted, I would call attention to the *exit*. Not only is the history of performance replete with any number of exits by actors across traditions, from the flamboyance of Kabuki to Nora's banging-of-the-door final exit in A *Doll's House*, one is reminded of the 'exit' that is built into the act of going to the theatre for any spectator. For every act of entering the theatre, there is an exit. If there is 'No Exit', then we are in Jean-Paul Sartre's envisioning of 'hell'.

Think of those exit signs, the four letters—EXIT—emblazoned in red against a black background, which invariably shine throughout a performance at strategic places in the auditorium. We tend to forget these letters even as they may be the only source of illuminated light in the darkened space. Most directors clamouring for a 'total blackout' know that it's almost impossible to get the administration of any theatre to switch off the Exit lights. That goes against the fire laws and imperils the very safety and protection of both the space and the people inhabiting it, including cast, crew and audience. And yet, the act of exiting the theatre could be one of the least pondered of all actions in theatrical discourse. Hypervisible, it also remains invisible, and does not seem to warrant any critical attention.

In contrast to the exit, so much has been written and mystified about the act of *entering* any theatre space, the sheer magic of inhabiting 'another world', which persists even when the work is anti-illusionistic or postdramatic. So much more has been reflected on the *duration* of any theatrical experience, not just in terms of its aesthetics but also in relation to the social interactions in the auditorium. These interactions used to be a lot more volatile and charged in earlier theatrical times, involving loud conversations, booing, flirtations and diverse forms of intrigue: think of social behaviour in the animated environments of the Elizabethan stage, the lascivious flirtations of Restoration theatre and early opera. Even in this sociological context, the act of exiting the theatre has hardly received any sustained theoretical or historical inquiry. It would seem as if the exit is too evanescent to be captured in words: the crossing of the threshold of the theatre into the world outside—a street, a subway station, a supermarket, an open field—remains relatively unmarked.

Many years ago, Peter Brook had raised a pertinent question: When the play ends, what remains? This question takes us into the realm of memory and public solitude, into debates and heated post-performance conversations at the bar, or else, into the oblivion of silence or the inner recesses of the unconscious, as one walks back home after a show. For academics, there is the post-performance, discursive world of reviews and commentaries that accumulate in archives which, for some critics, is extraneous to the essentially transitory, death-in-life phenomenology of theatre as an experience.[6] Of more crucial concern to me is another question that emanates from Brook's, but with a different inflection: When the play ends, what *begins*?

This is the interstice that is of unfailing significance to me: the in-between space that comes into being when a play comes to an end and something else is emergent that has the potential to begin or is in the process of beginning. Playing the devil's advocate, one could ask: Does anything begin? And, if so, how does one measure this beginning? Countering the illusory assumptions of many demagogues in the theatre, I would acknowledge that nothing

---

6 This position is argued by Peggy Phelan in *Unmarked: The Politics of Performance* (London and New York: Routledge, 1993).

of earth-shattering significance is likely to begin when a play ends—no overthrow of the government, no insurrection of the people—but, perhaps, there is something akin to a perceptual shift of energies in one's awareness of the world that manifests itself but at such an infinitesimal level that one is hardly aware of it.

To tease out some of these perceptual shifts, I turn first to a philosophical conundrum that underlies many premodern dramatic texts in the Indian tradition, even as it may be explicitly spelt out only in a few plays. I am referring here to a shift of consciousness that gets linked to the archetypal conundrum involving 'the snake and the rope' which pervades Indian philosophy but with particular reference to the school of Advaita (non-dualism) as propounded by Adi Sankaracharya (c.8th century CE). As philosopher Sundar Sarukkai has put it:

> The basic problem can be put as follows: when I see a snake (which later on I come to cognize as rope), am I not really seeing a snake? I see the snake and think it is real (so here is the connection between appearance and its reality). But when I realize it is a rope and see it as a rope, what does this say about my 'real' perception of the snake? The basic argument is that either the snake that I saw must have a real existence or it must have been non-existent. Since I saw the snake as clearly as I see a chair (and I conclude the chair is real), I must also conclude the snake is real. How then do I explain that it has become something else in my perception? I cannot say it was non-existent because my perception of it showed it as if it was real as something external to me.[7]

7 Sundar Sarukkai, correspondence with author, 22 September 2021. See Robert A. Goldman's perceptive article 'The Serpent and the Rope on Stage: Popular, Literary, and Philosophical Representations of Reality in Traditional India', *Journal of Indian Philosophy* 14 (1986): 349–69.

Following up on this argument that has been reiterated and debated over centuries, Sankara had argued that there is a third type of object that is neither existent nor non-existent. It is unde-terminable (*anirvacaniya*) insofar as it eludes being determined as either real or unreal. For Sankara, this becomes the model for understanding the reality of the world in his propagation of Advaita Vedanta. In this philosophy, the world is an illusion in all its multiple manifestations and errors of judgement, and there is only one consciousness in which Brahman (the Ultimate Reality) is identical to the Atman (the Inner Self).

At a more terrestrial level, one could argue that the act of exiting the theatre at the end of a performance has the potential to confuse, sublimate and complicate the nature of what is per-ceived as 'real' in everyday life. A rope could be mistaken for a snake, using these categories at a metaphorical level. And, in this confusion or arrival at a new category of thought, one could say that something has 'begun' which was not there prior to entering the theatre.

At another level, in engaging with more sensory performative experiences, I am reminded of the 'endings' of the iconoclastic plays staged by the Hungarian dissident group Squat, which enacted Dadaist and often obscene scenarios against the back-ground of a glass storefront on 23rd Street in downtown Manhattan. In these unforgettable experiences from the late 1970s, which form a collage of surreal fragments in my mind, I can never forget the unsettling experience of being mirrored and stared at by passers-by on the street who peered voyeuristically into the glass window of the store as the performance continued to be staged. During such moments, one often got the uncanny sensation that there were two audiences and that they were mir-roring each other like aliens. When one left the storefront theatre by the street door, inevitably to pounding music and irreverent lyrics, I would often experience something like a post-performance sensorium in which the street itself and everything on it—the street lights, the traffic signals, the garbage cans, the sirens of the police cars—were charged with a hyperreal intensity. The street was no longer the same street when I had entered the theatre; it was radically, spellbindingly transformed, and with that transformation, I was transformed with the implacable sense that something could begin.

If my description of this 'end-of-performance' experience is somewhat too ebullient, it can be related to the fact that it recalls a pre-pandemic experience of theatre, which still continues to live in mind and body as memory and sensation. With the outbreak of the pandemic and the unilateral closure of theatres, it could be said that we entered a state of permanent exit. Not 'No Exit', but 'Only Exit'. It is in recalling this state that I am compelled to think *beyond* theatre by invoking harsher manifestations of 'endings' and 'beginnings'. Through these manifestations what comes to life are larger mythical, ecological and cosmic narratives.

ON THE CUSP OF MULTIPLE TIMES

As I attempt to write about the ceaseless destruction of life in the 'second wave', it is uncanny how the intensity of this moment gets inextricably linked in my mind to the narrative of the Mahabharata, a connection that seems to be functioning at the level of the 'political unconscious' through a concatenation of historical, political and symbolic forces. Certainly, there is no literal connection, insofar as the epic in all its immensity does not refer to a pandemic at all. Nonetheless, it almost seems as if the Mahabharata is retelling or rewriting itself within the immediacies of this tumultuous moment.

Returning to the primary motif of the interstice which forms the leitmotif of this section, I would call attention to the radical shift in time that occurs towards the end of the Mahabharata narrative, as it hinges on the cusp of two *yugas*—the Dvapara Yuga and the Kali Yuga, which continues to this day. We are in the Kali Yuga, the Dark Age, which is marked by conflict, violence and death. To provide some background in order to better understand the implications of this 'cusp', the word yuga (literally, 'yoke') refers to an epoch, or an almost limitless expanse of time. Nonetheless, it is meticulously measured in years, thereby confirming the predilection in early Indian eschatology to *calculate* that which lies beyond the constraints of human comprehension. In actuality, as Romila Thapar has pointed out in her magisterial yet concise account of time as metaphor of history in early India, time is calculated at three levels—the divine, the ancestral and the human.[8] Therefore, in calculating the *mahayuga*, or the completion of four cycles of time—Krita, Treta, Dvapara, Kali—which are said to recur in that precise order, the total number of years in this cycle, as calculated in the realm of the gods, would be 12,000 years. But, in human time, this would amount to 4,320,000 years, which is how a *kalpa* gets defined as the longest period of time.[9]

To concretize what Thapar so perceptively describes as 'the fantasy of figures', there are any number of metaphors and visual ideograms in which impossible spans of time are cogently evoked. Thus, in the ancient Buddhist text of the *Saṃyutta Nikāya*, a kalpa is envisioned on these lines:

---

8 All reference to concepts of time in early India in this section are drawn from Romila Thapar, *Time as a Metaphor of History* (New Delhi: Oxford University Press, 1996).

9 Thapar, *Time as a Metaphor of History*, pp. 13–15.

If there is a mountain in the shape of a cube, measuring one *yojana* [two and a half to nine miles] and if every hundred years the mountain is brushed with a silk scarf, then the time that is taken for the mountain to be erased by the scarf is the equivalent of a *kalpa*.[10]

Far from nullifying the factuality of its actual duration in years, this kind of 'picture' enhances the factuality of the kalpa, thereby revealing that, in the early Indian framework of time, metaphor and the concrete could reinforce each other's sense of reality. Indeed, as David Shulman has pointed out in his insightful study of the imagination in South India, it is only when a phenomenon is fully imagined that it can be regarded as 'real', or 'more than real', far surpassing the evidence of verisimilitude.[11]

In a similar register, there is no dismissal of 'cyclical time' in early Indian cosmologies as *not* belonging to history; this viewpoint is more of an Orientalist judgement that got hegemonized by colonial powers during the modern age. Countering the notion that cyclicity is hopelessly ahistorical or anti-historical, Thapar points out how cyclicity and linearity can coexist in the measurement of time in early India and both can contribute to the reading of history.

More relevant to the discussion of the radical shift in the Mahabharata between the Dvapara Yuga and the Kali Yuga is the deterioration of *dharma* (law of righteousness) over the yugas.[12] While the Krita Yuga (also known as Satya Yuga) is regarded as utopian in its sense of plenitude, longevity of life, absence of

---

10 Thapar, *Time as a Metaphor of History*, p. 16.

11 David Shulman, *More Than Real: A History of the Imagination in South India* (Cambridge, MA: Harvard University Press, 2012).

12 All the facts in this paragraph are drawn from the section on 'Time and the Decline of *Dharma*' in Romila Thapar, *Time as a Metaphor of History*, pp. 21–5.

disease and division in society, the Kali Yuga, in which we are placed today, represents the darkest, the most conflictual and violent of times, where the burden of labour intensifies with the scarcity of resources. Significantly, from a contemporary Dalit or subaltern point of view, the ascendancy of the lower castes and the sexual freedom of women during the Kali Yuga can be seen as markers of celebration and hope rather than of doom. However, there is no glimmer of such celebration or hope towards the end of the Mahabharata when, following the eighteen-day war, the Dvapara Yuga segues into the Kali Yuga.

The end of the war results in the deaths not only of all the Kaurava brothers and almost the entire Pandava army but also of Krishna's clan, the Yadavas, who kill each other in a brawl following the curse of the sages.[13] Even as this annihilation of clans signifies something on the lines of 'the end of the world', it is important to keep in mind that what follows in the Kali Yuga is even more dark and brutal. In other words, it is fatuous to assume that the 'beginning' that follows a catastrophic 'end' is necessarily all sweetness and light. Rather, as in the case of the Kali Yuga, darkness deepens and the end of the world becomes increasingly more formidable and imminent.

* * *

---

13 The sages are provoked when Krishna's son, Samba, from his wife Jambavati, is produced before them disguised as a pregnant woman. Teased by Krishna's relatives whether Samba will give birth to a boy or girl, the sages pronounce that he will give birth to an iron club (*musala*). Even as this club is crushed to pieces and strewn into the sea, these pieces are washed to the shore where they grow like metallic grass. At some point, Krishna's clan of the Yadavas gets divided on a trivial matter and a battle ensues between the warring factions. In this battle, they use the grass as weapons only to realize that the grass has the lethal impact of an iron club. In the process, the Yadavas kill one another in a mindless rage.

What kind of 'cusp' could we (humans) be living in at the time of the pandemic? Without attempting to translate the cusp of the yugas into a contemporary discourse of history, Dipesh Chakrabarty provides a timely perspective in The Climate of History in a Planetary Age (2021) by arguing that 'we live on the cusp of the global and what may be called the "planetary".'[14] While the globe that we have been living with through our long-standing submission to the dictates of globalization is a 'humanocentric construction', the planet, or the Earth system, 'decenters the human'. Today it is no longer possible to restrict our understanding of the world to those forms of life that are identified exclusively as 'human'; one is compelled to acknowledge the infinitely more multitudinous forms of 'nonhuman' life on earth and in the larger planetary sphere. In the process, one is compelled to move beyond the 'limited timescale' which has determined our understanding of history in the world to include 'inhumanly vast timescales of deep history' inhabiting the planet. In essence, we have come to realize that the 'now' of 'human history' is inextricably 'entangled with the long "now" of geological and biological timescales', and this conjuncture, as Chakrabarty puts it bluntly, 'has never happened before in the history of humanity'.[15]

This cusp between the global and the planetary should not be treated as a binary, as Chakrabarty cautions, but as a mutually imbricated condition. It mirrors the shift between the Holocene epoch (c.11,700 years old) and the age of the Anthropocene, even as the latter term, so ubiquitous in critical discourse today, has not been uniformly accepted by all geologists.[16] Through the

14 Dipesh Chakrabarty, The Climate of History in a Planetary Age (Chicago and London: University of Chicago Press, 2021), p. 3.
15 Chakrabarty, The Climate of History, pp. 4, 7.
16 Chakrabarty, The Climate of History, p. 3.

onslaught of capitalism, biotechnology, extraction of natural
resources, industrialized agriculture and nuclear tests, driven by
a unidirectional and irreversible obsession with progress and
development, the Anthropocene signifies a new geological epoch
which has been directly affected by the human impact on 'the
earth's geology, chemistry, and biology.' In other words, humans
are no longer endowed with an agency to contribute to purely
material or humanist endeavours within the framework of the
'globe'; at a planetary level as well, they have been acting for some
time as a 'geological force'—destroying biodiversity and contributing to climate change and the emission of greenhouse gases.[17]

Reflecting on the intensification of greenhouse gases, one
study indicates that 'our climate has accumulated an amount of
heat equivalent to the explosion of four Hiroshima bombs per
second, totalling 2,115,122,880 bombs' from 1998 until 2014.[18]
From such formulations, it becomes clear that the statistical force
of figures has taken on a new dimension of threat, countering
the more genial interface of figures, concepts and metaphors in
reading expansive notions of time in early India, where a kalpa
could designate 4,320,000 years as well as a mountain in the shape
of a cube that would take that many years to be totally erased with
a silk scarf. In contrast, the calculation of heat through greenhouse
gases in relation to Hiroshima bombs opens up the omnipresent
lethal threat of Kali Yuga, with no signs of a return to the utopian
cycle of time commemorated in the Krita Yuga.

The brutal irony is that 'although [the Anthropocene] began
with us, it will end without us.'[19] We face the impossibly bleak

17 Chakrabarty, The Climate of History, p. 7, for both citations.
18 Déborah Danowski and Eduardo Viveiros de Castro, The Ends of the World
(Rodrigo Nunes trans.) (Cambridge: Polity, 2016), p. 5.
19 Danowski and de Castro, The Ends of the World, p. 5.

thought that 'the Anthropocene will only give way to a new geological epoch long after we have disappeared from the face of the Earth.'[20] In this sense, a post-Anthropocene scenario is a lot harsher to imagine than the crossing of the 'cusp' from the Dvapara Yuga to the Kali Yuga, as envisioned in the Mahabharata, not least because we are still alive in the Kali Yuga; this would not be the case in the post-Anthropocene age. Chakrabarty attempts to lighten the darkness of this moment by reminding us that, even as we face the prospects of extinction, there is still the possibility of human agency manifesting itself through all kinds of struggles. He further reassures us that the sheer violence on the planet and to planetary resources 'does not mean that the human phenomenological experience of the world is over'.[21] Nonetheless, it is a chilling thought to realize that in the post-Anthropocene age, there will be no such 'human phenomenological experience'— because we (humans) will have been extinguished by then.

GENOCIDE

Let me indicate two modalities of what could contribute to the shaping of a fatal end in our times. I will begin with genocide (Greek *genos*, 'race or people'; Latin *cide*, 'kill'), which is broadly understood as 'the intentional act to destroy a people—usually defined as an ethnic, national, racial, or religious group—in whole or in part'.[22] Once again it is in the Mahabharata that one encounters a genocidal impulse. In his robust reading of 'Murderous Rage

---

20 Danowski and de Castro, *The Ends of the World*, p. 5.

21 Chakrabarty, *The Climate of History*, p. 8.

22 For a background on the official definition of 'genocide', coined by Raphael Lemkin in 1944 and later adopted by the UN, see Office on Genocide Prevention and the Responsibility to Protect: available at https://www.un.org/en/genocideprevention/genocide.shtml

and Collective Punishment as Thematic Elements in Vyāsa's *Mahābhārata*' (2021), Robert Goldman draws on categories like 'ethnic cleansing', 'apocalypse' and 'mass-extinction' to list a number of dire events that affect not only the human but also the non-human world.[23]

Therefore, it is not insignificant that the epic begins with a snake sacrifice (*sarpasattra*) orchestrated by Janamajeya and directed against the entire snake population to avenge the death of his father Parikshit by snakebite. One is reminded in this context of the disproportionate scale of counter-terror attacks in our times, where the sheer onslaught of retaliation is legitimized on grounds of 'just war', which camouflages a thirst for revenge and incremental violence. Later in the Mahabharata, there is the 'mass extermination of creatures' (*bhūtānāṃ kadanaṃ mahat*) masterminded by Krishna and Arjuna as they burn the Khandava forest to appease the vengeful fire god, Agni.[24] Feminist scholar Iravati Karve has represented this carnage as divested of the basic 'rules of conduct': 'The sole aim was the acquisition of land and the liquidation of the Nagas.'[25]

When one attempts to take in these totally excessive forms of violence, one is compelled to remember that the war of the Mahabharata has a larger divine sanction. The very 'purpose' of the incarnation of Krishna, as the god Indra declares, is 'not only *jaya*

---

23 Robert A. Goldman, '*Ā Garbhāt*: Murderous Rage and Collective Punishment as Thematic Elements in Vyāsa's *Mahābhārata*' in Nell Shapiro Hawley and Sohini Sarah Pillai (eds), *Many Mahābhāratas* (Albany: SUNY Press, 2022), pp. 37–52.

24 Goldman, '*Ā Garbhāt*', p. 46.

25 Iravati Karve, *Yuganta: The End of an Epoch* (New Delhi: Sangam Books, 1974), p. 104.

(victory) but a literal cleansing of the earth (*bhuvah śodhanāya*)'.[26] So, in facilitating the transition between the Dvapara Yuga and the Kali Yuga, Krishna has the task of exterminating all the kings of the Dvapara Yuga, whose excesses have become too extreme for the Earth Mother to bear. While this appeasement of the Earth Mother's grief is the usual rationale for all *avatars* to unleash violence before returning to their celestial abode, one is struck by the sheer genocidal imperative of Krishna's mission. Goldman gets to the roots of this genocide when he describes this 'extermination of the warrior class not only down to the last man, but, as it is often described, *ā garbhāt*: "down to the very embryos in the womb".'[27]

No character epitomizes this genocidal temperament more explicitly than Ashwatthama, who seeks revenge for his father Drona's death following the subterfuge played on Drona by Yudhishthira in the battlefield that his son had been killed. Intrinsically related to Ashwatthama's genocidal act is the availability of divine weapons—the Narayanastra, or the weapon of Vishnu, and the Brahmastra, the weapon of Brahma.[28] The former has the capacity to unleash 'millions of deadly missiles simultaneously, the intensity of which rises in proportion to the resistance of the target'. Fortunately, Krishna, as the incarnation of Narayana, is fully aware of how this deadly weapon unleashed by Ashwatthama against the Pandava army can be resisted through mass non-resistance and surrender. *En masse*, the Pandavas lay down their arms in what would seem like a strategic form of nonviolence. In the process, they save their lives—because the

---

26 Goldman, '*Ā Garbhāt*', p. 41.

27 Goldman, '*Ā Garbhāt*', pp. 41–2.

28 All the information relating to the weapons in this section are drawn from Wikipedia entries on Astra (weapon); Narayanastra; Brahmastra; and Brahmashira [Brahmashirsha].

Narayanastra has no power against such a surrender of violence. Tellingly, if the Narayanastra is used for a second time, the weapon can only destroy the user's own army. In this way, Ashwatthama is checkmated by Krishna who knows the weapon's limitations more clearly than the young and impetuous warrior.

Setting aside the dimensions of military strategy, defence, counter-defence and the logic of deterrence that can be read in this narrative of weapons, I will focus on the second and more lethal weapon associated with Ashwatthama, the Brahmastra, that enters the narrative after he has succeeded in slaughtering the Pandava army in a night-raid. Not content with this carnage, Ashwatthama then resolves to kill the Pandava brothers with the Brahmastra. Losing control, Krishna advises Arjuna to fire the anti-missile, the Brahmashira, to counter the Brahmastra. In this potentially apocalyptic war of weapons which would surely result in the end of the world, it is left to Vyasa, author of the Mahabharata, and the sage Narada to intervene. They command Ashwatthama and Arjuna to withdraw their weapons. While Arjuna is in a position to withdraw the Brahmashira, Ashwatthama is not in a position to take back the Brahmastra. In what has to be regarded as one of the most heinous of murderous actions in the slaughterhouse of the Mahabharata, Ashwatthama uses the Brahmastra to target the unborn foetus in the womb of Uttara, the widow of the warrior Abhimanyu who has been slaughtered on the battleground.

At this critical juncture, it is Krishna who expresses his most unconditional rejection of meaningless brutality that goes against all the norms of the dharma of war. Mercilessly, he tears the divine talismanic gem from Ashwatthama's forehead, leaving behind a gaping, bleeding, festering wound, which can never be healed— Ashwatthama is cursed to endure his lonely, friendless and despised existence in our Kali Yuga, with no end in sight. As a counter-gesture, and perhaps one of the very few life-sustaining moments in the Mahabharata, Krishna revives the baby in Uttara's womb. The baby grows up to be Parikshit, whose son Janamajeya becomes the first auditor of the Mahabharata when he requests a bard to tell him what happened during the war.

I bring up these details from the Mahabharata narrative to point out that a genealogy can emerge out of the deadliest of genocides, thereby suggesting something along the lines of a 'happy end'. However, this is nothing short of a brutal illusion, because the narration of the Mahabharata that follows through Janamajeya's initiative is scarcely conciliatory or nostalgic; it has been designed to provide a story-telling diversion to the real intention of the snake sacrifice—the extermination of snake gods (*nagas*) and their terrestrial kin. In the course of the narration of the Mahabharata through 18 books, the decimation of kings, clans and unnamed soldiers is elaborated, as it continues to be reiterated in our times through numerous retellings, reminding us of the 'real' Mahabharatas that continue to be fought with brutality and hatred in the world.

Drawing on Ashwatthama's ruthless crime of targeting an unborn child, one is reminded of the virulence of foeticide in our times, which has been institutionalized in India for generations through customary patriarchal practices that prefer boys to girls. More recently, in the modern age, the abortion of female foetuses has been practised under the pretext of checking the health of the foetus.[29] This has resulted in the deliberate murder of millions of

---

29 See the entry on amniocentesis in Wikipedia for the normative uses of amniocentesis in contrast to G. B. Kaur, 'Female Foeticide: A Danger to Society'—*Nursing Journal of India* 87(4) (April 1996): 77–8; available at https://bityl.co/Avz0—where the focus is on the misuse of amniocentesis for the abortion of unwanted female foetuses.

unborn female children in India, who are part of a larger global population of 'more than 100 million missing women' as pointed out by economist Amartya Sen in a famous article published in 1990.[30]

On a lesser scale, but no less virulently, foeticide has also featured in genocides on minorities, as in the Gujarat pogrom against Muslims in 2002, where instances of foeticide have been documented as affirmations of communal hate. Among the numerous crimes of sexual violence against Muslim women, including 'forced nudity, mass rapes, gang-rapes, mutilation, insertion of objects into bodies, cutting of breasts, slitting the stomach and reproductive organs, and carving of Hindu religious symbols on women's body parts',[31] perhaps the most despicable crime was the one inflicted on Kausar Bano, who was nine months pregnant. As her sister-in-law, an eyewitness to the crime, testified: 'They cut open her belly, took out her foetus with a sword and threw it into a blazing fire. Then they burnt her as well.'[32]

While a women's fact-finding team has acknowledged that there were many variations in the details of the violence inflicted on Kausar Bano, as testified by other witnesses, the report confronts these variations in a bold and mature reflection:

---

30 Amartya Sen, 'More Than 100 Million Women Are Missing', *The New York Review of Books*, 20 December 1990 (available at https://bityl.co/Avz8). Sen's study extends beyond the large number of deaths resulting from the abortion of female foetuses to include larger social, economic and political factors contributing to the general neglect of women in relation to healthcare, nutrition, education and social services, as well as widespread instances of violence against women resulting in their deaths.

31 Quoted in Harsh Mander, 'One Thing Was Distinctly Rotten about 2002 Gujarat Riots: Use of Rape as a Form of Terror', *The Print*, 24 April 2019: available at https://bityl.co/AvzE

32 Siddharth Varadarajan, *Gujarat: The Making of a Tragedy* (New Delhi: Penguin, 2002), p. 229. The source of this statement is Saira Banu, Naroda Patiya at the Shah-e-Alam Camp, 27 March 2002.

Were these simply the fevered imaginings of traumatized minds? We think not. Kausar's story has come to embody the numerous experiences of evil that were felt by the Muslims of Naroda Patiya. [. . .] In all instances where extreme violence is experienced collectively, meta-narratives are constructed. Each victim is part of the narrative; their experience subsumed by the collective experience. Kausar is that collective experience—a meta-narrative of bestiality; a meta-narrative of helpless victimhood.[33]

The targeting of a woman's body and foetus remains intact in a relentless cycle of violence against women.

Against the sheer brutality of such evidence of genocide, it is hard to imagine how there can ever be something like a resurgence of humanity. At such moments, which are almost impossible to theorize, one can only fall back on those odd illuminations of human resilience and rejuvenation that one may have encountered in a stray encounter or conversation. Many years ago, following a long and exhausting blockbuster conference in Taiwan on the 'rebirth of the traditional arts in Asia', I remember sharing with a small group of participants my discomfort with the word 'rebirth', which had a Born-Again connotation for me. Why was it not possible, I argued, to focus on re-invention?

To this question I will never forget the response that I got from a Cambodian curator in the group who intervened by saying, 'But for us in Cambodia, whatever we are experiencing today in the arts is a rebirth.' He was referring to the atrocities of the Khmer Rouge under the dictatorship of Pol Pot whose ethnocide was so

---

33 Farah Naqvi, Ruth Manorama, Malini Ghose, Sheba George, Syeda Hameed and Mari Thekaekara, 'The Survivors Speak', *Outlook*, 2 May 2002: available at https://bityl.co/Avzl

brutal that it almost seemed as if nothing would survive his killings but a 'tower of skulls'.[34] I am drawing here on an image used by Rabindranath Tagore in his evocation of Japanese atrocities during the Nanjing massacre. Indeed, these skulls have survived in war museums that memorialize the Cambodian genocide in the master narrative perpetuated by Holocaust museums whose primary rationale is to ensure that such atrocities never happen again. Listening to the curator talk about the efflorescence of songs, dance, music and art gaining a new lease of life in Cambodia today, I was duly chastened. And so, I am compelled to acknowledge that such a renewal of life, art and culture is nothing short of a 'rebirth'.

EXTINCTION

Along with the genocidal impulse, one needs to point out the ecocidal drive that has resulted in the near extermination of the environment and the nonhuman species. As Deborah Bird Rose, Thom van Dooren and Matthew Chrulew have pointed out in their formative intervention on *Extinction Studies: Stories of Time, Death, and Generations* (2017): 'More than 99.9% of all species that have ever existed in the history of the planet are now extinct.'[35] This is such a sobering, if not impossible, figure to grasp that it compels us to accept the discomfiting truth that we (humans)

---

34 In his acerbic correspondence with Japanese nationalist Noguchi Yonejiro, who defended the Japanese atrocities on China during the Second World War as 'the war of Asia for Asia', Tagore had reminded Noguchi that, 'You are building your conception of an Asia which would be raised on a tower of skulls.' For more on the Tagore–Noguchi correspondence, see my *Another Asia: Rabindranath Tagore and Okakura Tenshin* (New Delhi: Oxford University Press, 2006), pp. 168–71.

35 Cary Wolfe, 'Foreword' in Deborah Bird Rose, Thom van Dooren and Matthew Chrulew (eds), *Extinction Studies: Stories of Time, Death, and Generations* (New York: Columbia University Press, 2017), pp. *vii–xvi*; here, p. *vii*.

perpetuate our lives in oblivion of those species living in the air, the earth and the ocean. We either take them for granted or we participate in their liquidation for the gratification of our own material needs and illusions of development.

To whom does it matter after all to ask: 'When a being, human or nonhuman, dies, what goes out of the world? What is lost to the world? And what world are we left with?'[36] It is significant to point out here that the loss being addressed here is a 'loss for the world' in all its immensity; it is not just a personal or social or political loss that is directly linked to what Chakrabarty would describe as a 'humanocentric' concern. Rather, we are attempting to address the idea of 'loss' at a planetary and nonhuman level. In this context, it would be hard to imagine any registration of loss among most people for the Honshu wolf or the Tasmanian tiger, among other extinct species. What does it matter after all if they disappear?

While in the 'heat dome' of western Canada in early July 2021, the deaths of 500 people in British Columbia were duly reported, along with hundreds of wildfires, what was scarcely a source of concern was the incineration of *more than a billion* marine animals in the intense heat.[37] Such is the ignorance, if not indifference, of most humans to ecocidal catastrophes at an aquatic level. We simply get on with our lives by killing and eating animals, destroying forests for the building of housing estates and parks, building dams and unified river systems, among other civilizational pursuits of progress and development.

As the world faces its 'sixth mass extinction event'—unique in relation to the earlier extinction events insofar as it is 'being driven almost entirely by humans'—scholars of extinction studies call our

---

36 Wolfe, 'Foreword', p. *viii*.
37 Reported by Leyland Cecco from Toronto in '"Heat Dome" Probably Killed 1 BN Marine Animals on Canada Coast, Experts Say', *The Guardian*, 8 July 2021: available at https://bityl.co/AvzL

attention to the fact that extinction is '*never* a generic event'; it impacts millions of species in highly individuated and context-specific ways.[38] At times a species 'may *already* be said to be extinct even though the last survivors of its kind live on', as in the case of the passenger pigeon.[39] Deborah Bird Rose refers to this condition as a 'deathzone: the place where the living and the dying encounter each other in the presence of that which cannot be averted'.[40] This could be the most painful interstice to imagine, an in-between space and time when 'death is imminent but has not yet arrived'.[41] While we may experience this trauma at a very personal level in observing and experiencing the dying of a loved one, the scale of this dying for the nonhuman species occurs at a mega level that far exceeds the level of human comprehension.

Among the axiomatic home-truths about extinction pointed out by Rose, van Dooren and Chrulew, it is important to keep in mind that extinction signifies 'a collective death, the end of a living kind'.[42] It has a profound impact on 'intergenerational heritages', so much so that it represents 'the irreparable disruption and destruction of the *generativity* of such generations'.[43] Above all, it calls to attention to the clash of multitudinous times, ranging from the 'deep-time processes of evolution and speciation' to the 'frighteningly rapid pace at which biodiversity loss is today taking place'.[44]

---

38 Wolfe, 'Foreword', p. *viii*.

39 Wolfe, 'Foreword', p. *xi*.

40 Wolfe, 'Foreword', p. *xi*. Quoting from Deborah Bird Rose, 'In the Shadow of All This Death' in Jay Johnston and Fiona Probyn-Rapsey (eds), *Animal Death* (Sydney: Sydney University Press, 2013), pp. 1–20; here, pp. 3–4.

41 Rose, 'In the Shadow of All This Death', pp. 3–4.

42 Deborah Bird Rose, Thom Van Dooren and Matthew Chrulew, 'Introduction: Telling Extinction Stories' in *Extinction Studies*, p. 8.

43 Rose, Van Dooren and Chrulew, 'Introduction', p. 9.

44 Rose, Van Dooren and Chrulew, 'Introduction', p. 9.

In today's world of technoscience, this 'frighteningly rapid pace' needs to be related to an almost manic obsession with speed. Just think of our own impatience, bordering on rage, when our computer systems happen to be running a few seconds slow. Significantly, this exposure to the acceleration of speed is a late-twentieth-century phenomenon with philosophers like Paul Virilio specifically coining words for new fields of thought—such as 'dromology'—in order to engage with the 'science of speed'.[45] Such a science is particularly applicable in the context of new technologies of war where drones can be used to target individuals in faraway spaces and the speed of light can be matched by laser weapons and computer-controlled weapons systems. So infinitesimal is this capitulation to speed that it 'risks normalizing,' as Richard Beardsworth puts it, 'an experience of time that forgets time.'[46] In other words, a nullification of time by the sheer speed of time itself.

Ironically, it is this preoccupation with speed that necessitates a new calibration on our part of 'the different *speeds* of different forms of life'.[47] All is not lost as some humans, however small in number, can continue to think, as Chakrabarty has reminded us, against the grain of extinction. In this regard, Wolfe puts it perceptively when he calls to our attention 'the slowness of the leatherback turtle, the speed of the viral vector or the bacterial network, the immense sonic architectures by which humpback whales reconfigure time and space on a literally global level'. Significantly, these 'differential speeds [. . .] express themselves

---

45 Paul Virilio, *Speed and Politics: An Essay on Dromology* (Mark Polizzotti trans.) (New York: Semiotext[e], 1986).
46 Richard Beardsworth, *Derrida and the Political* (London and New York: Routledge, 1996), p. 148. Quoted in Wolfe, 'Foreword', p. *xii*.
47 All citations by Wolfe in this paragraph are from 'Foreword', p. *xii*.

in us', and, most significantly, as Wolfe acknowledges, we are only just beginning to understand them.

There is something humbling about this acknowledgement of different modalities of time as we come to terms with the axiomatic fact that 'human time' is just *one* mode of understanding temporality. There are other times as I have indicated in my brief account of early concepts of time in early India, which would include ancestral time and divine time. Today, through new calibrations of knowledge relating to the posthuman or nonhuman world, we need to let go of the hubris of human time dominating all other times, and explore new forms of living in and with slow time. In other words, along with the deadening terror of extinction that pervades our lives, whether or not we are fully aware of it, there is also the possibility of discovering new temporalities of existence and survival.

HIROSHIMA MUSEUMIZED: APORIAS OF PEACE

This dyadic understanding of the terror of extinction coexisting with new temporalities of life is what I would like to focus on now by calling attention to a paradigmatic example of extinction: the atomic bombings of Hiroshima and Nagasaki on 6 and 9 August 1945, respectively, whose cataclysmic explosions have contributed to the Anthropocene in no small measure. Some years ago, while visiting the Hiroshima Peace Memorial Museum, I remember wandering in numbed silence through the main assembly hall, taking in the relics, artefacts and testimonies of the survivors. Past the clock with its hands frozen at 8.15 a.m., the exact time of the atomic bomb explosion, I remember thinking how the museum had succeeded in capturing the sense of time standing still even as it was driven by the dual purpose of memorializing and mourning the dead, and making its visitors think about the deadly consequences of nuclear power.

At one point, I walked past a nondescript photograph of bamboo plants, nothing spectacular, a seemingly neutral image whose caption caught my attention. I don't remember the exact words but it said that when Ground Zero emerged in the hypocentre, the point of origin of the nuclear blast, it was assumed that nothing would ever grow in this concentration of nuclear ash. And yet, years later, bamboo shoots began to sprout from the ash, testifying to the almost miraculous power of the resurgence of nature.

I remember my eyes being blinded with tears as I found myself recalling Tagore's undying faith in the endurance of nature to withstand the most mechanical forms of violence. This comes through, for instance, in his defiant assertion as a poet that 'in a little flower, there is a living power hidden in beauty which is more potent than a Maxim gun.'[48] At one level, this is a seemingly quaint and archaic reference to the 'Maxim gun', the first 'recoil-operated machine gun in the world that was invented in 1884, the first automatic firearm in the world'.[49] Compared with the atomic bombs used in Hiroshima and Nagasaki, it appears to be anachronistic even as it had the capacity to kill. Yet one is struck by Tagore's quiet determination that the destruction of such a gun cannot match the silent 'living power' of a flower.

What would Tagore have said about the atomic blasts in Hiroshima and Nagasaki? Fortunately, perhaps, Tagore did not live long enough to know about these events even as he had written some of his most devastating critiques of Japanese imperialism during the Second World War in his exchanges with the ultra-nationalist Noguchi Yonejiro, a former friend with whom he had once shared an affinity for Romantic poetry. I have written in my book *Another Asia* about this broken friendship haunted by Tagore's

---

48 Quoted in Bharucha, *Another Asia*, p. 93.
49 See the Wikipedia entry on Maxim gun.

quasi-Orientalist love for Japan, the Land of the Rising Sun embodying the Spirit of Asia, which got systematically shattered by the warmongering enterprise of the Greater East Asia Co-prosperity Sphere.[50] It was through this military construction that Japan attempted to impose its ultra-nationalist and imperialist power over other Asian nations.

Hypothetically, I am not sure what Tagore would have felt about the assertively modern and internationalist architecture of the Hiroshima Museum and Memorial Park, emphatically influenced as it is by the severe architectural lines and functionalist aesthetics of Le Corbusier. Significantly, in a fact that is not often recognized, Kenzō Tange, architect of the Hiroshima complex, had earlier designed the Commemorative Building of the Greater East Asia Co-prosperity Sphere in 1942, almost 13 years before the Hiroshima Peace Memorial Museum was opened to the public.[51] It would be hard to imagine two more disparate blueprints commemorating war and peace.

In a blatant affirmation of nationalism in the context of a Japanese-style modern architecture, Tange had defended his rationale for the 1942 Commemorative Building by saying: 'We must ignore both Anglo-American culture and the pre-existing cultures of the Southeast Asian races. To admire Angkor Wat is the mark of an amateur.'[52] It is very unlikely that Tagore would have responded to that remark kindly. And yet, such are the paradoxes by which traditional Japanese principles of space can be

---

50 See Bharucha, *Another Asia*, pp. 168–73.

51 See the Wikipedia entry on Kenzō Tange for background on his considerable range and achievements as an architect.

52 Quoted by Hyunjung Cho, 'Hiroshima Peace Memorial Park and the Making of Japanese Postwar Architecture', *Journal of Architectural Education* 66(1) (4 December 2012): 72–83; here, p. 74.

embedded and transformed in the overwhelming concrete of the Hiroshima Peace Memorial Museum that it is hard to deny Tange's achievement.

Perhaps, the conceptual power of the Museum's *raison d'être* is most powerfully rendered in what is recognized as the Memorial Cenotaph, a saddle-shaped monument that frames the Peace Flame and the A-Bomb Dome, perhaps the most iconic image of what continues to remain of Hiroshima after the blast in the 'skeletal ruins of the former Hiroshima Prefectural Industrial Promotion Hall'.[53] Against these ruins, what gets foregrounded is the Peace Flame, which has burned continuously since it was lit in 1964. This Flame represents a beacon of hope for a nuclear-free world at the same time as it is a flame of protest—it will continue to burn until all nuclear weapons have 'disappeared from the earth'.

One could argue that the Peace Flame occupies an interstice insofar as it invokes a tragic past and an as-yet-unrealized future. The past in a sense is still with us, it has not yet passed, and the future has not yet arrived as a premonition in the present. Rather like one of Kafka's protagonists, we are caught in a 'gap' between past and future, as Hannah Arendt has reminded us in her memorable study of *Between Past and Future*.[54] The one limitation of her model of two forces of time colliding with each other and deflecting at the point where a human figure stands in their path, is its unquestioned universality. In attempting to connect this

---

53 For all references in the following paragraphs to the Memorial Cenotaph and the Peace Flame, see the Wikipedia entry on Hiroshima Peace Memorial Park.

54 For all references to the 'gap', as theorized on the basis of one of Kafka's parables, see Hannah Arendt, 'Preface: The Gap between Past and Future', *Between Past and Future: Eight Exercises in Political Thought* (London: Penguin Classics, 2006), pp. 3–16.

interstice—or 'gap', as Arendt would put it—to the larger moment of the pandemic in which we are placed, I would suggest that regardless of the omnipresence of the pandemic at a global level, it has significantly impacted countries and peoples. We are all caught between past and future in radically different ways. The impact of the pandemic cannot be restricted to epidemiological considerations; it has to be perceived in relation to a cluster of complex cultural, aesthetic, political and religious considerations that are not part of the mainstream discourse on the pandemic.

So, with this perspective in mind, I would risk stretching the political implications of the Peace Flame by making something of a philosophical detour in calling attention to how that flame affects me as a Parsi Zoroastrian. With no exaggeration, Zoroastrians as a community are so minuscule in number that the community has often been viewed within the larger framework of 'extinction'.[55] There is a larger social context to this reality of shrinking numbers that is not relevant to the discussion here. But, at a more philosophical level, one could argue that intrinsic to the rituals of Zoroastrianism is the worship of fire. This does not make us fire worshippers, as is commonly believed. Rather, what

---

55 From a report published in the *Hindustan Times*, 17 April 2006—'Parsis May Become Extinct By 2070?', available at https://bityl.co/Aw0O—we learn that the population of Parsis in India was 100,096 in 1901 with a growth rate of 6.33. By 1941 the growth rate was 5.08 and, according to the 1951 census, 'there was a negative growth rate of –2.7 per cent.' After Independence, there was a regular decline in the population with the growth rate as low as –21.52 per cent in 1981. The general trend indicates that by 2070 the population of the community will be zero.

At a more personal level, I should acknowledge that my larger apprehension of 'extinction' during the pandemic was, perhaps, at an unconscious level, heightened by the fact that there are around 400 Parsi Zoroastrians in my home city of Kolkata, who continued to die with alacrity of COVID-19, among other diseases, during the pandemic.

is worshipped is the *atash*, the sacred fire which burns continuously in our temples, which is not the personification but the purest and most auspicious symbol of Ahura Mazda.

There are different gradations of fire in Zoroastrian ritual practices insofar as the most auspicious of temples, notably *Atash Behrams* (Fire of Victory), consecrate a particularly auspicious fire which contains fires from at least sixteen different sources, ranging from the fire retrieved from the houses of potters, brickmakers, ascetics, goldsmiths, ironsmiths, to more elemental forms of fire as produced by lightning and the carefully retrieved embers from a funeral pyre.[56] At an unconscious level, I find myself connecting this sacred history of the atash to the Flame of Peace in Hiroshima, even though, technically, one could debate whether an electrical or gas-induced fire can be regarded as holy in the Zoroastrian context.

This is the aporia that confounds me: On the one hand, nothing could give me more joy and a profound sense of relief, if not exhilaration, than if the Peace Flame could be extinguished because that would mean, at an impossibly utopian level, that all nuclear weapons have ceased to exist in our world. On the other hand, there is this underlying disquiet operating in the inner recesses of my mind as a Zoroastrian, that this extinguishing of the flame would mean nothing less than the end of the world. In effect, I find myself caught between wanting the Flame to be extinguished once and for all, and seeing in its flickering existence

---

56 For a listing of the different kinds of fire used in the sacred *atash* of the Atash Behram, see https://en.wikipedia.org/wiki/Atash_Behram. For scholarly studies on Zoroastrian religion, see Mary Boyce's classic study, *Zoroastrians: Their Religious Beliefs and Practices* (London: Routledge, 2000) and the first part on Zoroastrian religious teachings, ecclesiastical history and ritual practices included in Pheroza J. Godrej and Firoza Punthakey Mistree (eds), *A Zoroastrian Tapestry: Art, Religion, and Culture* (Ahmedabad: Mapin, 2002).

the undying hope of a nuclear-free world even as nuclear power continues to threaten the peace of the world.

I never imagined that in writing about the pandemic I would be articulating such a thought, but it has so happened that through the atrocities of ecocide, which is what took me in the direction of Hiroshima in the first place, such thoughts have emerged unexpectedly.

Having travelled in this section of the narrative through early concepts of time in ancient India mediated by the terror of the Mahabharata into reflections on genocide and ecocide, let us now return to the moment of the pandemic and ask more direct questions of ways of coping with it and learning to live with ourselves.

THE ETHOS OF WAITING

How do we position ourselves today in what appears to be an interminable ending of the pandemic to which there seems to be no end? Different countries appear to be positioned in different temporalities as they come to terms with the pandemic in their own ways. As the 'second wave' has already segued into the 'third wave', I find myself recalling the 'first phase' when the virulence of the 'second wave' had not yet registered. During the first lockdown beginning in March 2020, I found myself turning to Samuel Beckett's *Waiting for Godot*, which remains unsurpassed for its theatricalization of the ethos of waiting. No play, to my mind, captures so relentlessly the phenomenology of waiting in which two tramps on a country road, Vladimir and Estragon, wait for someone called Godot who never shows up.

You can read whatever you want to in the figure of 'Godot' depending on your circumstances and location. Prisoners, for instance, in several prison complexes across the world, waiting to be released on life sentences, are likely to read the possibilities of impossible freedom while enacting Beckett's play in the prison itself. In the life imprisonment of their sentences, Beckett has offered them ways of imagining new beginnings for themselves. Eliciting and yet defying all interpretations of the play, it is best to take Beckett seriously when he says: 'I don't know who Godot is. I don't even know (above all don't know) if he exists. And I don't know if they believe in him or not—those two who are waiting for him.' And then, with his characteristic wit and impatience in dealing with hermeneutic demands, he adds: 'Maybe [the characters] owe you explanations. Let them supply it. Without me. They and I are through with each other.'[57]

With such an emphatic rejection of attempting to 'fix' Godot as an entity, human or nonhuman or divine, it would be hazardous to see in Godot any allusion to the end of the pandemic, any more so than it would be appropriate to see his most crystallized 35-second intermedial, anti-representational, anti-illusionistic play titled *Breath* as a premonition of the pandemic. In this fragment of a play, divested of the live presence of a single actor, on a stage littered with rubbish, the *mise en scène* (if this is the appropriate word for a total absence of movement) is structured around recordings of an 'inspiration' and 'expiration' of breath juxtaposed with two identically recorded sounds of a newly born child. It would be hazardous to read in this most abstracted temporality any allegory around life and death, or even the disappearance of time: one can only 'breathe' its duration of 35 seconds in 'live time' and submit to the experience.[58]

---

57 One of the many exasperated statements made by Beckett in response to the ceaseless search for meaning and interpretation in *Godot*, included in https://theatrenetwork.ca/culture/history-of-godot/
58 The most inspired and interdisciplinary study of *Breath* is Sozita Goudana's book *Beckett's Breath: Anti-theatricality and the Visual Arts* (Edinburgh: Edinburgh University Press, 2018), where the play is a springboard for a

Against the acute brevity of *Breath*, *Godot* explores the almost unbearable tedium of *waiting* enacted on stage by at least four main characters. It is the time taken to wait, the games played during the waiting, the intermittent moods of despair, solitude, resignation, irreverence and occasionally boisterous humour that give the play its distinctive performative register. Beckett, one could say, provides us with a template for waiting. And yet, as a dramaturg, I do remember that before the pandemic was on the horizon, when it was possible to travel almost incessantly, I found myself questioning at that time why Estragon and Vladimir needed to wait at all. Why don't they just exit at the end of the play and leave the audience with an image of a bare stage? Surely that would be a more provocative and thought-provoking end than this needless ritual of waiting?

That, I would submit, was a pre-pandemic thought. During the pandemic, however, I realized that my imagined exit of Vladimir and Estragon at the end of the play was just a clever, dramaturgical idea. Today I am convinced that they have no other choice but to wait. Whether they continue to wait with Godot in mind is another matter. I don't wish to equate our condition in the pandemic with this Beckettian predicament, but confined to our houses for eighteen months on end, with no possibility of travel, I have come to realize that there can be no short-cuts in the condition of waiting.

---

spectrum of reflections on breath-related artworks in performance art, new media, painting and sound art. For the insight on seeing *Breath* in the larger context of 'live performance', I turn to Corey Wakeling's nuanced reminder in *Beckett's Laboratory: Experiments in the Theatre Enclosure* (London: Methuen Drama, 2021), p. 154: '*Breath* remains live insofar as a breathing audience registers it. Without the provisionality of time in which the work plays out, it would be a work of installation art whose duration would be merely elective, and the expiration of the work no longer structurally important.'

Today, as I continue to wait in my apartment in Calcutta, as lockdowns have been imposed and lifted, as the street outside my house has exploded from silence into cacophony with the frenzied celebration of the Pujas and, more recently, Christmas, I think that we have no option but to look upon waiting as a condition, a time-pass duration, with ups and downs, highs and lows, a fluctuating energy, held together by an underlying discipline. Not the discipline of 'scientific management' or 'Taylorism' that was introduced in the late nineteenth century to enhance the efficiency and productivity of industrial labour,[59] nor the Foucauldian discipline imposed on us by the governance and the surveillance of the postcolonial state, one needs another epistemology of 'discipline' to free its possibilities of self-realization from apparatuses of power that produce docile citizenship and a compliant labour force.

Perhaps, one needs to turn to the inner discipline practiced by Gandhi through any number of crises and political disturbances, during which he constantly reinvented different experiments with his inner self, ranging from fasting to silence. In this regard, it is worth recalling that during the Spanish flu pandemic, when Gandhi was laid up in bed not with the flu but with dysentery, that he refused to pursue everyday activity, admonishing everyone around him for their irresponsible movement: 'The body of the person who has chosen to follow the dharma of service must become as strong as steel as a result of his holy work. Our ancestors could build such tough bodies in the past. But today we are reduced to a state of miserable weakness and are easily infected by noxious germs moving about in the air.' Countering

---

59 The clearest exegesis of 'scientific management' in relation to the idea of 'performance', as explored in Performance Studies, is Jon McKenzie's *Perform or Else: From Discipline to Performance* (London and New York: Routledge, 2001).

the assumption that a militant satyagrahi should always be ready to 'act', Gandhi affirms a different counter-strategy in the context of the pandemic: 'There is one and only one really effective way by which we can save ourselves even in our present broken state of health. That way is the way of self-restraint or of imposing a limit on our acts.'[60] 'Saving ourselves' through a containment of movement rather than a reckless defiance of the virus is another kind of discipline that is expected of a 'true warrior'.

Even if one accepts these onerous conditions of waiting—and I realize that this may not be a desired option for many of my readers—one is compelled to ask: Waiting for what? One may attempt to de-signify 'Godot' of any meaning but it is harder to let go of the preposition 'for'. During the last months of the 'first phase' of the pandemic, it was very clear that we were Waiting *for* the Vaccine—that elusive panacea of all global woes which raced to come into existence, defying all earlier medical protocols of testing and producing vaccines over a period of years. Today, in record time, there are any number of vaccines available for use, at least in most parts of the world. Some countries with First World economies have been accused of hoarding an excess of vaccines, or worse, of wasting them, even as many poorer countries in the world have yet to vaccinate even a minuscule percentage of their populations. Inequities have intensified as greed and paranoia have become only too evident in fuelling the war of the vaccines that constitutes yet another Mahabharata of our times.

In this condition, there are tensions and conflicts between the haves and the have-nots, the vaccinated and the non-vaccinated (including belligerent anti-vax constituencies, often linked to right-wing and religious fundamentalist agendas). There are

---

60 Both citations are from Madhavankutty Pillai, 'The Virus That Killed 18 Million Indians', *Open Magazine*, 6 September 2018: available at https://bityl.co/Aw0h

disagreements between governments and corporations, between the manufacturers of vaccines and patent holders, between those who are free to travel and those who cannot (even though both parties may have been vaccinated with the same vaccine under a different name). These restrictions on travel can be regarded as a new form of racism not just against 'foreigners' but, at times, also against the citizens of a particular country who may be refused permission to return to their own 'homes'. The most virulent disparities in the War of the Vaccines exist among the vaccines themselves, which are hierarchized, valorized or demeaned on the basis of their countries of origin and affiliations to corporate brands.

In this regard, what comes to mind is a wicked meme that circulated widely during the first phase of the pandemic, just when the vaccines were beginning to make their presence felt on the global stage. There is a visualization of four male characters: Under the strapping figure of a white bodybuilder, a monolith of muscle and power, one reads the name 'Pfizer'. Alongside is a metrosexual guy, with a lean, gym-trained body, exuding coolness and strength. He is identified as 'Moderna'. Beside him—and you have to lower your gaze to see him—is a small, brown-skinned, South Asian man, bare-bodied and potbellied, with gold chains and amulets around his neck. Wearing dark glasses and holding a snack in one hand, he is identified as 'AstraZeneca' (also known as Covishield in my part of the world). And, finally, taking up all the space beneath these three men on top of the meme is an outrageous caricature of a man who seems to have run amok from an amateur production of Gogol's The Inspector General. With broken teeth and a drunken aura as he raises what appears to be a glass of vodka in his hand, he is marked as Sputnik-5.

All of this can be read as a joke. But it is a joke whose premises are clearly embedded in racial stereotypes, which could lie at the heart of the new racism that seems to be controlling and restricting the right to travel across the borders of the world. The reality is that travellers with less sanctified vaccines may not be able to travel at all, or may be compelled to submit to the most onerous quarantine regulations. Rewording Hobbes, I would say that our lives are becoming 'solitary, poor, nasty, brutish' and unbearably *long* as days are accumulating into months into years, as the pandemic shows no signs of ending in these conditions of deteriorating global uncivility.

While the illusion of normalcy may prevail sporadically, in fits and starts, here today gone tomorrow, the reality is that the pandemic cannot end so long as it continues to exist in some part of the world. In this sense, it is an inexorably interconnected global phenomenon. As its very etymology suggests—*pan* 'all', *demos* 'people'—a pandemic is not an epidemic that can be confined within particular regions and national borders. Nor can it be conveniently regarded as 'endemic' (literally, 'in the population'), which could be a euphemism used by governments eager to prove to their citizens that the pandemic is under control, even as foreigners are not particularly welcome to disturb the precarious equilibrium at home. The reality underlying these shifty arguments is that what exists *beyond* the borders of a particular nation remains as potentially foreboding as what does not seem to be a matter of concern *within* national borders. Even when the pandemic does end globally, one can be sure that the variants of the coronavirus will continue to mutate in the years that follow. We will have no other option but to live with many more viruses yet to be born and this will involve a new understanding and acceptance—or summary rejection—of the ethos of waiting.

RECLAIMING THE VITALITY OF THE BODY

In this intensification of uncertainty between endings that continue to end and beginnings that have yet to begin, it would be useful not to valorise the regressive category of the 'normal' or to seek refuge in the even more glib neologism of the 'new normal'. Conceptualizing our present condition through the formative category of 'catastrophe without event', Eva Horn draws on Walter Benjamin's prescient observation: 'That things "just go on" is the catastrophe. It is not that which is approaching but that which is.'[61] We are *in* a catastrophe. Some critics would extend the formulation by saying that, 'We (humans) *are* the catastrophe.' It is this deadly and tenacious 'normal' that needs to be recognized and confronted as the very site and incubation ground of the pandemic, which has germinated over the years through capitulations to global capitalism and rampant consumerism. These capitulations in turn have been complicit in the silent engineering of global warming and climate change precipitated by violent shifts in the order of nature. Deforestation, industrial farming and genetic engineering have catalysed tipping points of disaster at infinitesimal levels by igniting new forms of zoonosis (literally, *zoon* for 'animal' and *nosos* for 'disease') through the jumping of viruses across species.

Focusing on bats, the most maligned of creatures who are said to have played a crucial role in the outbreak of the novel coronavirus, displacing pangolins who were earlier surmised to have served as a 'bridge' between bats and human bodies, the brutal reality, as Fahim Amir reminds us, is that 'we' (humans) have 'hunted down' bats, among other animals, in the 'most remote

---

61 Quoted from Walter Benjamin's series of fragments on 'Central Park' by Eva Horn in *The Future as Catastrophe: Imagining Disaster in the Modern Age* (New York: Columbia University Press, 2018), p. 7.

corners of the world' and 'swallowed up their habitats' through 'mining, plantation farming, and lumber depletion'.[62] In a chastening perspective, Amir encapsulates the interconnectedness of different forms of destruction in the bat world resulting in the outbreak of diseases:

> Stressed to death, the immune systems [of the bats] go haywire, turning them into chronically feverish bio-reactors. Hounded to death, [bats] swarm in search of asylum and end up near animals that are equally weakened by hunting or husbandry: ideal conditions for chains of viral transmission. In eastern Australia, for instance, bats learned to live in trees near horse pastures (leading to Hendra virus). In Malaysia they turned up in the vicinity of an up-and-coming hog industry (Nipah virus). In Saudi Arabia, where animal farming had changed over from nomadic to sedentary, they took up residence in camel stalls (MERS).[63]

If the pandemic has taught us anything, it is the utter foolishness and arrogance of 'absolutiz[ing] the otherness of nonhumans' without recognizing how intimately the animal world intersects with our own.[64] As we continue to territorialize and destroy their environments, or kill them in large numbers without realizing the consequences on our ecology or economy, we have only ourselves to blame.

---

62 Fahim Amir, 'A Touch Too Much: Animals of the Pandemic' in Ekaterina Degot and David Riff (eds), *There Is No Society? Individuals and Community in Pandemic Times* (Essen: Verlag der Buchandlung Walther Konig, 2020), pp. 157–73; here, p. 162.
63 Amir, 'A Touch Too Much', p. 161.
64 Amir, 'A Touch Too Much', p. 163.

As many writers, social scientists and political economists have pointed out, it is the global forces of the economy, extraction of minerals, the food industry, tourism and rampant consumerism that have impacted on the planetary energies sustaining both the human and nonhuman worlds. So, if better sense could prevail, this should be a time of self-reckoning by recognizing the severity and irreversibility of an ongoing catastrophe that cannot be circumvented through a mere submission to the 'new normal' which amounts to nothing more than a structural adjustment of existing discriminations and disparities. Nothing less than a new way of 'inhabiting the planet' is needed because, as Achille Mbembe puts it, 'This Earth is our shared roof and our shared shelter. Sharing this roof and this shelter is the great condition for the sustainability of life on Earth. We have to share it as equitably as possible.'[65] While at one point in time we could afford to be preoccupied with 'how life emerges and the conditions of its evolution', the key question today is 'how it can be repaired, reproduced, sustained and cared for, made durable, preserved and universally shared, and under what conditions it ends'.[66]

While seeking new ways of 'inhabiting the planet' is too large an agenda for this particular narrative to address, let me focus on one particular site that has not been adequately confronted in emergent planetary discourses where the human body has been conspicuously marginalized as a link to planetary energies. While much has been written about Gaia as the 'living earth'—an earth

65 Achille Mbembe, 'Thoughts on the Planetary: An Interview with Achille Mbembe', New Frame, 21 September 2019: available at https://bityl.co/Aw15. See also Milo Rau in conversation with Achille Mbembe, 'The Paranoia of the Western Mind' in There Is No Society? Individuals and Community in Pandemic Times, p. 132.
66 Mbembe, 'Thoughts on the Planetary'.

that is not merely a breathing, vital force of ever-renewing energies but also a being that suffers and is capable of retaliating with anger against the depredation of its resources—the intervention that I would like to make here is that Gaia is not an entity, however vital, *outside* ourselves: it is a potential force *within* our bodies.[67]

While Amitav Ghosh in his magisterial yet urgent reflections on a 'planet in crisis' invokes the principle of Gaia, he acknowledges that it may be 'impossible to regain an intuitive feeling for the Earth's vitality once it has been lost', or if it has been 'suppressed, through education and indoctrination'.[68] In this crisis, the only concrete means of retrieving this lost connection, for him, would seem to be entirely discursive. Even at this level, he is aware that 'written accounts of Gaian conceptions of the world' are hard to find because those who are in touch with the forces of 'non-human vitality', notably shamans immersed in indigenous modes of knowledge, have been 'largely silenced, marginalized, or simply exterminated'.[69] This is only too true but, perhaps, it is not through the 'written word' alone that one can inhabit the living energies of Gaia. I would suggest that the spirit of Gaia is more likely to live in the non-verbal, embodied, and psychophysical languages of dance, music and song. So, while I am in total agreement with

---

67 See Amitav Ghosh, *The Nutmeg's Curse: Parables for a Planet in Crisis* (New Delhi: Penguin, 2021) for references to the mythology of Gaia, pp. 85–90, which he develops in the larger context of the principle of vitalism.

68 Ghosh, *The Nutmeg's Curse*, p. 205.

69 Ghosh, *The Nutmeg's Curse*. Ghosh pays tribute to one of the few written testaments that we have of indigenous beliefs in relation to the planetary crisis by analysing Davi Kopenawa and Bruce Albert's *The Falling Sky: Words of a Yanomami Shaman* (Nicholas Elliott and Alison Dundy trans) (Cambridge, MA: Belknap Press, 2013). Originally published in French in 2012, this book is the outcome of a long collaboration between shaman/indigenous leader Kopenawa and French anthropologist and activist Albert.

Ghosh that 'nonhuman voices' need to be 'restored to our stories',[70] I would add that nonhuman energies of the most potent nature can animate our bodies through vital energies in non-verbal modes of representation.

If I appear to speak with some confidence about what would appear to be a rather elusive, if not invisible, resource of hidden energies, I would freely acknowledge that I owe this understanding to the visionary dance practice of Indian choreographer Chandralekha. Recognized for her uncannily intimate and sensual perception of the 'living earth' within the body, intimately linked to the disciplines of Yoga and the martial-art practice of Kalaripayattu, she was able to see how the most minute observations of nature, including animal, plant and insect life have been crystallized in the most abstracted of movements.[71] This holistic knowledge of the interconnectedness of different kinetic and visual traditions is what contributed to Chandralekha's understanding of *shariramandala*, the body as *mandala* or cosmic diagram. In this formulation, the body is linked to cosmic energies through inner disciplines of the body animated by the vital principle of femininity (*prakriti*).

Perhaps, in no moment of her choreography is the principle of *shariramandala* more vivid in its corporeality than her embodiment of Sakambhari, the herb goddess, whose primordial inscription is to be found in a Harappan seal where we see a geometric

---

70 Ghosh, *The Nutmeg's Curse*, p. 257. This, indeed, is the concluding statement of Ghosh's book based on the urgent realization that 'nonhumans can, do, and *must* speak' in the larger context of 'unrelenting, apocalyptic violence.'

71 For a biography of Chandralekha and the conceptual histories surrounding her dance practice, see my book *Chandralekha: Woman/Dance/Resistance* (New Delhi: HarperCollins, 1995).

abstraction of a female figure lying on the floor, legs outstretched upwards to the sky and a tree emerging from her *yoni*.[72] While a detailed analysis of this performance would not be appropriate here, suffice it to say that an extraordinary minimalist abstraction of Sakambhari opened Chandralekha's production of *Sri* on the empowerment and enslavement of women. This was followed by a group representation of the *matrikas*, earth goddesses, who are imagined to protect the earth but not divested of destructive powers as well. The purpose in embodying these figures was not merely to evoke images of powerful women in 'female-centred societies' in proto-historical times, but also to examine how their energies could be reclaimed in contemporary women's movements burdened by patriarchy and residual practices of disempowerment. Inimitably, in a language that was specifically her own, Chandralekha dared to ask: 'Can women realize that they are, themselves, Mother Goddesses?'

Significantly, the Mother Goddess that Chandralekha has in mind is not a beneficent and nurturing figure, a repository of reassurance. On the contrary, she is 'ferocious', to use one of the keywords used by Ghosh to describe the figure of Gaia. So ferocious, indeed, that figures like the *matrikas* had no difficulty in adorning their bodies with weapons. Why then do we call them 'mothers'? This was the question posed by Chandralekha to Professor H. D. Sankalia, Sanskrit scholar and archaeologist specializing in proto- and ancient Indian history. The learned professor had the honesty to acknowledge that he hadn't thought of the question earlier. For Chandralekha, this inscription of the 'mother'

---

72 See Bharucha, *Chandralekha*, pp. 317–26 for a brief description of how Chandralekha created the figure of Sakambhari in her production *Sri* within the larger framework of 'body as a preserver of history'.

could be most accurately read in relation to the self-generative capacity of figures like Sakambhari, both 'virgin and yet mother, as no father seemed necessary for the society in which she originated'.[73] Sakambhari rises from the earth herself, and unlike Gaia who has to deal with a jealous husband who is obsessed with stealing her children, Sakambhari is her own woman, resplendent and forever creative in her affirmation of the life principles and vitality of the earth.

Celebrating the 'fecundity principle' of mother goddesses with seeds, plants, leaves, shrubs and trees emerging from their bodies, Chandralekha was well aware of the rich evidence of their existence across the borders of India in temple sculptures, clay tablets and seals, descriptions in ancient texts and poems, apart from the gestures and movements of dance:

> She is seen as *Salabhanjika*, the tree goddess, surrounded by fruits, flowers, leaves.
> She is seen sitting erect and upright on the branch of a neem tree.
> She is seen moving out from a tree trunk with her arms outstretched.
> She is seen descending from a *Shami* tree.

---

73 Chandralekha, 'Who Are These Age-Old Female Figures?', *The Wire*, 8 March 2018: available at https://bityl.co/B4Wy. I am grateful to Sadanand Menon for calling my attention to this article, originally published in *The Economic Times* in 1991. The article opens with Chandralekha asking Prof. H. D. Sankalia why goddesses are designated as 'mothers'. In his correspondence with me on 14 January 2021, Menon has also linked Chandralekha's research on Sakambhari, the *matrikas* and earth goddesses to her 'extensive and country-wide research' for her exhibition on *Stree: Women of India* in 1988, part of the Festival of India in the Soviet Union. I have discussed this exhibition at length in *Chandralekha*, pp. 287–94.

PORTRAIT OF CHANDRALEKHA BY SADANAND MENON

She is seen striding in all directions, penetrating all
  points in space, before returning to the tree.
She is seen as a protector of fields and harvests; villages
  and children.
She is seen as a guardian against pestilence and disease.
She is seen as half-bird half-woman; half-serpent half-
  woman; half-tiger half-woman; half-tree half-
  woman.
She is seen as a composite form—a fluid movement
  between animal, human, plant.
She is seen on a crocodile or a fish in the midst of
  whirling waters.
She is seen as a water-goddess and a water pot.
She is seen as a jar of grains.[74]

Unabashedly poetic, Chandralekha did not speak the language of academia, even as she engaged with its discourses quite
closely. I would say that she spoke a 'dance language', which is
sometimes dismissed a bit too rashly by academics, including
feminists, as too 'metaphysical' or 'essentialized'. To work against
this possibility, I will now attempt to situate Chandralekha's
knowledge of the inner energies and vitality of the body in a
broader social and political context. I will begin by asking the
crucial question: How do we situate the body today in the age of
the pandemic? Can we find ways of rejuvenating it against the
pressures of disease, social anxiety and breathlessness? As our
lungs are being attacked and pollution intensifies, how do we find
ways of renewing our breath?

---

74 Chandralekha, 'Who Are These Age-Old Female Figures?'

STILLNESS AND MOVEMENT

In a state of deep disequilibrium, let us accept that it is time to pause and regain our balance. Choreographer and dance theorist André Lepecki would insist that we should reject the regimen of stasis, which merely replicates the lockdown surveillance of all movement monitored by the state. As he formulates the problem, in the 'social choreography being imposed on the general population', which hovers between '*suspension*' and '*stoppage*' of the 'normal flow of life', the consequence is that 'movement has been placed under house arrest'.[75] One should qualify at this point that this 'arrest' applies primarily to the privileged sectors of society, who can afford to stay at home, unlike the service sectors, the unemployed and the homeless who had no other option but to continue working during the pandemic, and for whom 'nothing has really stopped'. As Lepecki observes, in the worst days of the pandemic, the unemployed have had to wait for longer hours in 'not-so-socially-distanced lines' for their doles while the homeless continue to be on the run, in order to escape the intensified vigilance and persecution of the police and security agencies.[76]

In these constraints of movement for the underprivileged, it becomes essential not to unconditionally accept 'the management, surveillance and control of movement' by the police and the state authorities. However, in one's resistance to these constraints, the alternative is not to submit to the frenetic speed of neoliberal capitalism, which continues to underlie different states of confinement at a spectral level in the hard-wiring of our bodies to an array of technological devices. One can be 'wired' to all kinds of global

---

75 André Lepecki, 'Movement in the Pause', Rio de Janeiro, 21–28 June 2020. Available at: https://bityl.co/B4X2. I am grateful to André Lepecki for sharing the accurate weblink of this important article.

76 Lepecki, 'Movement in the Pause'.

networks and consumerist services while being stuck in one's room. Inevitably, the pandemic has exposed the double-edged phenomenon of 'movement' at both physical and virtual levels within the traps and deceptions of a neoliberal capitalist economy: On the one hand, it is through movement, as Lepecki argues, that 'one escapes disciplinary apparatuses of capture'; at the same time, 'it is also through movement that systems of power drill and break-in a subject into subjection'.[77]

In this impasse, where it would seem that we are caught between new forms of voluntary imprisonment and residual desires of kinetic freedom intensified by our immersion in virtual technologies, Lepecki makes a sharp manoeuvre—one that, I would suggest, could only come from a choreographer. He suggests—indeed, advocates—the exploration of a 'movement in the pause'. What makes this 'movement' so cognitively rich is that it embodies a 'stillness which is simultaneously refusal, potentiality, and action.'[78] At a temporal level, one also needs to keep in mind that this movement is uncompromisingly 'slow'.

Prana

I will hold on to both these motifs—a stillness that combines 'refusal, potentiality, and action' and 'slowness'—to turn to the one substantial choreographic body of work that I am personally acquainted with which seems to embody both these conditions. In the process, I will attempt to link psychophysical disciplines of the body to planetary energies. Returning to Chandralekha, with whom I had interacted for some years, I focus now on some moments during the process of her production *Prana*, which she

---

77 Lepecki, 'Movement in the Pause'.
78 Lepecki, 'Movement in the Pause'.

described as 'a homage to breath'.[79] Arguably open to 'utopian' ways of synergizing the body in relation to the world and the planet, Chandralekha was radical both in her life and work.[80] However, even as she was closely linked to a wide range of feminist and environmental movements, she never quite belonged to these constituencies. Her visionary practice of resistance was ultimately anchored in the secrets of the body. And, as she would put it mournfully, most activists have 'damaged their bodies' and, even more critically, she believed that they had 'lost their spines'.

While Chandralekha has passed on, leaving behind a torrent of memories and insights among a wide range of dancers and feminists, I do believe that she would be delighted by Lepecki's choice of words in seeing 'stillness' as an amalgam of 'refusal, potentiality, and action'. In her choreography, which was steeped in the primary energies of Yoga, the performance of stillness was embodied in slowly evolving *asanas*. For her, *asanas* were not 'poses' (a word she despised); rather, they were better understood as 'circuits of energy'. In her production *Prana*, which was first staged at her open-air Mandala space on Elliots Beach in Chennai, she inscribed in her choreography the traditional *mandala* of the Navagraha, the nine planets in the Indian cosmological system, including two

---

79 The production of *Prana* has been described in some detail in my book, *Chandralekha*, pp. 217–36. The clearest exposition of *prana* comes from B. K. S. Iyengar, *Light on Yoga* (London: Unwin Paperbacks, 1989), p. 21: 'Prana means breath, respiration, life, vitality, wind, energy or strength [. . .] *Ayama* means length, expansion, stretching or restraint. *Pranayama* thus connotes extension of breath and its control. This control is over all functions of breathing, namely, (1) inhalation or inspiration, which is termed *puraka* (filling up); (2) exhalation or expiration, which is called *rechaka* (emptying the lungs); and (3) retention or holding the breath [. . .] which is termed *kumbhaka*.'

80 For an exploration of the 'utopian' dimensions in Chandralekha's conceptualization of the body, see my article 'Contextualizing Utopias: Reflections on Re-mapping the Present', *Theater* 26(1–2) (1995): 32–49.

eclipses (Rahu and Ketu). Each of these *grahas* was embodied through meticulously choreographed yogic asanas—each planet/ eclipse being represented by a specific numeral and icon.

So, Surya (Sun) was represented in all its solitary splendour with a circle; Soma (Moon) was represented by two dancers embodying the figure of the crescent; Angaraka (Mars) was repre- sented by a triangular formation through the numeral three; Budha (Mercury) was held as a droplet with four dancers, and so on. Each of these iconographic constellations was performed to the legendary *navagraha kritis* of Muthuswamy Dikshitar, which are considered to be among the most sublime compositions in the Carnatic music tradition. Between each embodiment of the grahas through asanas, there were intersections of movement in Bharatanatyam which exposed the most fundamental *adavus* (dance steps) in this dance vocabulary to the rhythmic non-verbal syllables of *sollukattus*: this was Chandralekha's classic way of 'stretching' the spatial dimensions of her choreography and 'cleaning the space', as she would put it evocatively.

All these glimpses of her work may seem overly formalist, with the asanas performed/danced in pure stillness. But in this stillness, there was always a slowly evolving movement—there- fore, the reference to Lepecki's 'movement in the pause' becomes apposite. The real test in performing the movement of the asanas was their extreme slowness (each segment of movement per- formed in *vilambit kaal*, the slow speed, which is rarely used in Bharatanatyam performances today where the focus is on speed and virtuosity). Having witnessed any number of rehearsals of *Prana* as it evolved, I can testify that it made impossible demands on the bodies of the dancers, in so far as each asana—it could be *vriksha* or 'the tree' (where the performer stands on one leg with the other tucked into the thigh, the hands raised above the shoulders) or the back bend of the *chakrasana* ('the wheel') or *urdhva dhanurasana* ('upward bow')—would have to be so meticulously paced that the movement would take almost *five minutes*. In dance time, this can be an eternity. The idea was not to 'arrive' at the movement in a virtuosic instant, but to show its 'journey'. This is what contributed to the moment-by-moment phenomenology of seeing planets come into being through the bodies of the dancers.

There is much more that needs to be said about the sheer rigour of Chandralekha's minimalism and the politics of her aesthetics which rested on the belief that the activation of vital energies coiled within our bodies can enable us to 'cope and confront', in her words, 'the daily assaults on our senses, and the unprecedented degradation of our bodies'. *Prana* is the release of these 'vital energies' in whose slowly evolving beauty there is also resistance to all forms of social and political conditioning. As Chandralekha often put it, if your spine is not fully energized, you will not be able to find the capacity to resist or to act. For her, political consciousness could not be restricted to the mental strategies of ideology or analysis, or to the purely pragmatic decisions of activism; it had to be embodied in an awareness of the body through the spine by recognizing how prana as a vital energy emanating from the base of the spine facilitates the fundamental act of breathing in a larger connection with the cosmos. Translated into our everyday life context, I would acknowledge that it is this act of self-conscious and controlled breathing that has become more critical than ever before as the coronavirus has attacked our lungs. Our survival then is directly related to an awareness of the renewal of breath, not just at a philosophical level but also in practice.

Oxygen

There are many examples of how 'breath' gets represented in the theatrical *oeuvre* but I will pass them over for the moment to focus on an altogether different kind of practice that is resonant with the work of Chandralekha. In this practice, breath and Yoga, stillness and resistance, come together through the act of freediving or breath-holding diving. Some explanation is needed for what might seem like a totally irrelevant, if not fantastic digression on my part. I first became aware of freediving, a contemporary 'sport' following in the tradition of Greek sponge fishermen, Polynesian pearl divers and Japanese *ama* (divers), when I participated in an inter-continental, inter-disciplinary project called Fluid States organized by Performance Studies international (PSi).[81] As part of the dramaturgical structure of this 'fluid' conference, structured around different performative interventions in different locations of the world, the idea was to send a 'vessel' from one 'port' to another in the nature of a gift.

So, based as I was in land-locked Delhi, where I had completed a conference at Jawaharlal Nehru University on 'rethinking labour in the creative economy' from a performative perspective, I was faced with the task of sending a message to the next port of call which happened to be Dean's Blue Hole in the Bahamas. This location with an unusual name is the world's second deepest

---

81 *Fluid States*, which was subtitled *Performances of UnKnowing*, was an exploratory attempt to decentralize the format of the blockbuster conference under the auspices of PSi. Functioning in different clusters in several parts of the world throughout the year 2015, I was the director of one such cluster that focused on a conference titled *Rethinking Labor and the Creative Economy: Global Performative Perspectives*, at Jawaharlal Nehru University, New Delhi.

FACING PAGE: WILLIAM TRUBRIDGE DIVING. PHOTOGRAPH BY LOUSIA JANE.

water-filled sinkhole and the site of one of the most important freediving competitions in the world. While the intrinsic connections between 'performance' and 'sport' in the vocabulary of Performance Studies was the reason why this freediving competition was included in *Fluid States*, the organizers justified their choice through their creative affirmation of a 'genuinely water-bound examination of performance' where, at conceptual and metaphorical levels, it placed its research '*within* the water, within a liquid space'.[82]

For me, this space also exemplified a rigorous testing ground to examine the potentiality of breath—breath that pushes the limits of human endurance to the very limits of existence, reminding one of Artaud's fundamental premise that 'there can be theatre only from the moment when the impossible really begins'.[83] Taking a cue from this reminder of the 'impossible' and drawing on the concept note of the organizers, I found myself sending a message from India to the Bahamas that was premised on 'what lies beyond the reach of breath'. This took me on an illuminating journey whose insights I will attempt to link at an implicit level to the earlier section on Chandralekha's more terrestrial journey of the body in relation to the cosmos.

In order to prevent the possibility of succumbing to what could be regarded as New Age metaphysical mushiness, let us turn to the words of William Trubridge, the world champion of free-diving who has dived 102 meters into the depths of the water. His

---

82 See the section on Dean's Blue Hole on the website of *Fluid States*: https://www.fluidstates.org. I am grateful to Sam Trubridge, director of the project at Dean's Blue Hole, for his generous insights into the project and also for introducing me to his brother William, who features prominently in my narrative.

83 Antonin Artaud, 'The Theatre and the Plague' in *The Theatre and Its Double* (Mary Caroline Richards trans.) (New York: Grove Press, 1958), pp. 27–8.

startlingly lucid book *Oxygen: A Memoir* (2017) can be regarded as a manifesto of the yogic discipline that goes into the act of breathing through an altogether unprecedented generation of prana.[84] Before turning to Trubridge, however, just keep in mind that freediving exists without any supplementary protective devices like fins or inflatable lift bags, still less an oxygen tank. The only concrete object is a rope that one is allowed to touch only once on one's return from the depths of the ocean, after retrieving a white disc with tags that has to be brought up to the surface of the water as proof of one's journey. Otherwise, all that exists is the body of the diver and his or her capacity to generate oxygen without any external supply of oxygen.

Now let's turn to Trubridge, beginning with the first moments of the dive itself:

> You suck in a last critical breath of air. It's a breath that's going to have to be your life support system for the next several minutes.
>
> Your body jackknifes upside down, your arms sweep the water and pull you under, and straight away, you feel the pull of your own buoyancy tugging you back to the surface, holding you back, asking you, Do you really want to go?[85]

This is the phase of the dive when one 'burns' the most oxygen, so it becomes imperative not to use too much energy, but to 'swim as quickly and powerfully to overcome that force'.

84 William Trubridge, *Oxygen: A Memoir* (New Zealand: HarperCollins, 2017, ebook).

85 I quote extensively in this section from William Trubridge, '"This Is Why I Free Dive": A Journey Into the Deep', TEDxChristchurch, 22 October 2018. Text prepared by Amanda Chew and Peter van de Ven. Available at https://www.youtube.com/watch?v=-MZetpFw7qY

Gradually, the surface lets you go. Inside your body, your lungs are compressing due to the pressure of the water column above you, and by 10 meters, [the lungs] are already half the volume that they were on the surface, meaning that the average density of your body has increased. When your density matches exactly the density of the water outside your body, then you're neutrally buoyant.[86]

As one descends, one has to let go of any sense of anticipation of one's arrival. Abandoning the memory of being terrestrial, one becomes 'aquatic'. The ocean is now one's 'home', and the deeper one merges with it, the more 'relaxed' one becomes.

The 'surface', as Trubridge reminds us—and this is what makes him a lot more than a daredevil sportsman—is not just the planetary surface, or the surface of the water, but also 'the surface boundary in our minds that separates the rational, conscious mind from the subconscious below.'[87] Anyone who practices meditation or mindfulness can enter that 'still sea'.

You become stillness immersed in stillness, and in that void, what is revealed is [. . .] an awareness of presence and presence in awareness. It's pure consciousness; it's the one thing that we may never ever be able to explain with science.[88]

On the long and treacherous journey back to the surface of the water during which time you have to 'pay' for 'the free ride down', as Trubridge puts it with his self-deprecating humour, you have to stop asking questions like, 'Have I gone too far?', or 'How

---

86 Trubridge, 'This Is Why I Free Dive'.
87 Trubridge, 'This Is Why I Free Dive'.
88 Trubridge, 'This Is Why I Free Dive'.

many more strokes do I need to get to the surface?' One's concentration lies elsewhere:

> Suddenly, your thoracic muscles contract, expanding your ribcage—it's an involuntary breathing reflex, trying to suck air into your mouth, but your mouth and your glottis stay clamped shut while you're underwater, so no water passes; and instead, your diaphragm is yanked up under your ribcage.[89]

Through all these strenuous, death-in-life moments, which could result in a fatal blackout, one lives in the moment. As the light returns finally on the surface of the water, the body regains its buoyancy.

I have consciously chosen to quote Trubridge at length because what he is experiencing cannot be easily summarized—it is not so much a 'representation' as pure movement. Besides, as a practitioner par excellence, he is extremely lucid about the relationship between oxygen, breath and blood, which is often complicated in more academic writings:

> Holding the breath means stopping the intake of oxygen. From that point on, the freediver depends on the oxygen contained within the body: mixed with other gases as air in the lungs; attached to haemoglobin (inside red blood cells) in the blood; and stored in myoglobin within muscle tissue. As the apnea (breath-hold) continues, these stores of oxygen become depleted.[90]

Trubridge attributes his capacity in resisting the depletion of oxygen to the unconscious lessons that he has derived from his

---

89 Trubridge, 'This Is Why I Free Dive'.
90 Trubridge, *Oxygen*, p. 8.

personal adaptation of Yoga where the purpose of the *asanas* and the flowing movement (*vinyasa*) is to purify the nerve channels (*nadis*) so that energy can travel more freely through the body. It is this energy which can be likened to prana that enables one to push the limits of breathing to another state of pure consciousness.

If all these details sound a bit too technical, perhaps it is best to turn to a more pensive language which Trubridge is as capable of expressing as his more precise self-reflexive observations on the minutiae of freediving: 'Be quiet now, be still and let that deeper part of you, the part that has always been and always will be, before birth, and after death, let that take you and bear you up.'[91]

Between 'before birth' and 'after death', one is opened not just to an interstice, but to something akin to a *kalpa*, a seemingly immeasurable length of time that I had brought up earlier in the context of ancient Indian concepts of time. And yet, the lesson that one learns from Trubridge traversing what seems to be an 'impossible' distance is that this journey is crossed in a continuous moment. This submission to the moment is made possible from the very start, when 'we leave a part of ourselves' as we dive through the surface of the water into its depths, leaving behind 'our history and our hopes', even 'the concept and memory of breathing'.[92] What exists is an energy animating another state of being that continues its journey regardless of its outcome or expectation or failure or possible death.

I offer these insights on the limits of body, breath and consciousness, as a point of reference against which I am compelled to return to the terrestrial world of breathlessness, which constitutes the central condition of our times.

---

91 Trubridge, *Oxygen*, p. 349.
92 Trubridge, *Oxygen*, p. 297.

Breath, Breathlessness and Combat Breathing

To bring the narrative back to theatre, breathlessness is the dramaturgical premise of a play that is almost too eerily relevant to the condition of the pandemic today. Caryl Churchill's dystopian radio play *Not Not Not Not Not Enough Oxygen*, first broadcast on BBC Radio 3 in March 1971, fantasizes an oxygen-deprived England which has been reduced to 'the Londons' in 2010.[93] Scarily, we have already crossed that dystopian moment in 2022, as we retrieve this sliver of a one-act play today from its largely forgotten history. The past and present temporalities of the play make it at once oddly prescient and terrifyingly nostalgic. Churchill's theatricalization of a dystopia that has already passed but is still in the process of being lived and may even have deepened is a reminder of something on the lines of a post-Anthropocene condition. However, as I emphasized earlier, no humans would be alive in the post-Anthropocene condition, whereas in Churchill's *Not Not Not Not Not Enough Oxygen*, the three characters are more or less alive, even as they have to purchase oxygen in order to breathe.

Breath-deprived, they are destined to remain confined in the claustrophobic confines of one-room apartments in tower blocks, where the air outside is so foul, the atmosphere so dense with toxins, that it's best for the windows to be shut at all times, with periodic sprays of oxygen in the room to enable its inhabitants to breathe. In this shattered ecology, it is rare to see a bird. The blue of the sky is a forgotten memory, and the grass in the much-coveted park area with a plethora of cottages is almost entirely depleted. Contributing to the dystopia of environmental degradation, if not total burn-out, there is an oppressive capitalist

---

93 Caryl Churchill, 'Not Not Not Not Not Enough Oxygen' in *Shorts* (London: Nick Hern Books, 2008, ebook).

system that commodifies all possible social and human relations, including the right of women to have children or an abortion. This capitalist network controls the most basic resource of survival, notably the commodification of oxygen, which makes the act of living possible but at a cost.[94]

In this dystopian world, Mick, aged sixty, with some memories of what the world was like before 'the Londons' became the norm, is waiting for his son Claude in the company of Vivian, his neighbour. She is married and would like to move in with Mick but he doesn't think that he can share his space. Claude, who is some kind of media celebrity, arrives in a state of exhaustion and collapses, having walked to his father's apartment. Instead of offering his somewhat opportunistic dad a large amount of money that could enable Mick to relocate to a cottage, Claude announces that he has given away all his money and is proceeding to opt out of the totalitarian capitalist system of 'the Londons'. In opting out of the system, Claude is following the path of his mother (Mick's estranged second wife), who has chosen to live in 'the wilderness' while accepting the possibility of starvation. At the end of the play, there is a suggestion that Claude joins the 'fanatics' (as Vivian brands those who are protesting against the system, killing others and immolating themselves). In the last image, in one of the few images of hope that somewhat deflects a totally dystopian present,

---

94 For a more detailed summary of Churchill's play within the larger context of the ecological dimensions of her vision, read Sheila Rabillard, 'On Caryl Churchill's Ecological Drama: Right to Poison the Wasps?' in Elaine Aston and Elin Diamond (eds), *The Cambridge Companion to Caryl Churchill* (Cambridge: Cambridge University Press, 2009), pp. 88–104. A nuanced perspective on Churchill's socialist feminism can be read in Elaine Aston, 'Caryl Churchill's "Dark Ecology"' in Carl Lavery and Clare Finburgh (eds), *Rethinking the Theatre of the Absurd: Ecology, the Environment, and the Greening of the Modern Stage* (London: Bloomsbury, 2015), pp. 59–76.

Mick invites Vivian to share his apartment as they both settle down to watch the announcement of Claude's death on television.

A thoroughly bleak play, I would acknowledge, that is permeated with both dark humour and socialist rage. What is of immediate concern to the condition of 'breathlessness' that has initiated my brief inscription of the play into the discussion is the language that Churchill creates for Vivian. She seems to be the most stricken of the three characters as she barely manages to find the breath to hold her thoughts together. I quote just one passage that captures some of the splenetic, broken and totally disoriented lines spoken by Vivian as she imagines that Claude has come to kill her and Mick:

> I knew knew always knew fanatic fanatic would come and kill, always saying millions dying hunger dying war hunger war every day so we kill die kill too and shock shock into stopping but doesn't stop, saying die kill die leaving rooms blowing up blowing blocks shooting self burning self shooting own family or stranger strangers in the street on the news and I switch off I switch I switch off but now I can't and I'm glad glad no more waiting do so it kill me do kill me now and it over get it over.[95]

What appears to be extreme neurosis is embodied in a language that is catalysed by the absence of breath. Vivian does not have enough oxygen to order her thoughts and speak clearly. Her language is excruciatingly breathless.

* * *

---

95 Churchill, 'Not Not Not Not Not Enough Oxygen', p. 60.

Shifting the time frame of this discussion back to the present of the pandemic, it would be useful to return to Franco Berardi, who initiated this section on 'endings and beginnings' and who reminds us that we live in an age of chronic breathlessness. With or without the pandemic, this condition has been with us for some time and is likely to stay. In his meditative polemic on *Breathing: Chaos and Poetry* (2019), Berardi argues that the metaphor of poetry could be 'the only line of escape from suffocation'. As the agencies of chaos in the social world have '[paralysed] the social body' and '[stifled] breathing into suffocation', he affirms that 'only poetry, as the excess of semiotic exchange, can reactivate breathing'.[96] While my narrative cannot elaborate on the redemptive force of poetry as it comes to the end of its own attempt to engage with breath at performative and social levels, I share Berardi's crucial insight that breathlessness cannot be separated from different forms of suffocation in political life.

This 'suffocation' is not just perceptible in our times; it has perhaps always existed in dealing with different states of brutality, particularly in relation to earlier and ongoing histories of colonization. In this regard, we need to be reminded of how Frantz Fanon in *The Wretched of the Earth* (1961) uses the terms 'suffocated', 'hemmed in', 'smothered' and 'imprisoned' to describe the dehumanizing experience of the colonized.[97] More powerfully, in envisioning the corporeal state of dehumanization, he calls attention to the phenomenon of 'combat breathing' imposed on the colonized. In a key passage from A *Dying Colonialism* (1965), Fanon expresses his position with distinctive clarity:

---

96 Franco Berardi, *Breathing: Chaos and Poetry* (Cambridge, MA: Semiotext(e) Intervention Series 26, 2019), p. 10.
97 Frantz Fanon, *The Wretched of the Earth* (Richard Philcox trans.) (New York: Grove Press, 2005).

There is not occupation of territory, on the one hand, and independence of persons on the other. It is the country as a whole, its history, its daily pulsation that are contested, disfigured. [. . .] [U]nder these conditions, the individual's breathing is an observed breathing. It is a combat breathing.[98]

What becomes vividly clear is that there is no hiatus between the colonization of the country and its psychophysical impact on the bodies and psyches of the colonized. Through its network of 'surveillance, monitoring, and control', as Joseph Pugliese has argued, the colonial state can be said to 'invade, in capillary fashion, the very psycho-physiology of the individual'. In the process, 'combat breathing' is doubly 'observed'—both 'by the state and the individual who has internalised this scopic regime'.[99]

So, on the one hand, it is possible to see 'combat breathing' as that which is imposed by the State on the colonized who find it 'impossible to breathe.' On the other, it is possible to see 'occupied breathing' not just in the context of what is imposed on the colonial subject; rather, one could argue that the individual's breathing is 'occupied in opposing the colonial occupation' through a 'clandestine form of existence', if not covert dissemblance and 'trickery'.[100]

---

98 Frantz Fanon, *A Dying Colonialism* (Haakon Chevalier trans.) (Ringwood: Pelican, 1970), p. 50.

99 Joseph Pugliese, correspondence with author, 5 October 2021. I am grateful to Pugliese for sharing his incisive views on Fanon so generously. As one of the key scholar-activists in the larger contexts of state surveillance and biopolitics, he is best known for his books *Biopolitics of the More-Than-Human: Forensic Ecologies of Violence* (Durham: Duke University Press 2020) and *State Violence and the Execution of Law: Biopolitical Caesurae of Torture, Black Sites and Drones* (London and New York: Routledge, 2013).

100 Karthick Ram Manoharan, correspondence with author, 8 October 2021. See his monograph *Frantz Fanon: Identity and Resistance* (New Delhi: Orient Blackswan, 2019).

'Combat breathing', therefore, has a double-edged agentic force in Fanon's activist thinking that that needs to be ceaselessly kept in mind

At one level, the psychosomatic condition of colonization can result in the disfigurement of the colonized, which can be directly related at a physiognomic level to the constraints on the colonized body whose symptoms include 'systemic contraction, muscular stiffness'. Walking becomes a 'shuffle'; it becomes impossible to 'bend'. In this 'atrophied' state, the 'patient' (as Fanon designates the colonized) hovers between 'life and death' as life is placed 'on hold'.[101] All these symptoms prevent the body from 'acting' in the most physical and transformative sense of the word. 'To live is to act,' as Stephanie Clare summarizes this condition, calling attention to the fact that 'action is not defined as transcendence over the immediate, immanent bodily conditions necessary for the reproduction of life. Instead, action is life's expansion, its self-transformation, and its engagement with the material world.' Rejecting any essentialized notion of 'the African body', which is inherently strong and resilient in its primordial power, Fanon had no patience with the imagined resources of the past as he envisioned life as 'future oriented', with individuals shaping and bringing about their own futures through militant action.[102]

In recent years, the concept (and practice) of combat breathing has been invoked by a range of political activists as they call attention to the conditions of brutality imposed on them and the oppressed sectors of society. In a particularly incisive evocation and analysis of combat breathing, the Australian activist-artist-poet Omeima Sukkarieh of Lebanese origin re-incarnates the struggle

101 Quoted in Stephanie Clare, 'Geopower: The Politics of Life and Land in Frantz Fanon's Writing', *Diacritics* 41(4) (2013): 60–80; here, p. 63.
102 Clare, 'Geopower', pp. 63 and 64, respectively.

of peace activists as they survive the onslaught of bombs and bullets:

> Breathe in through your nose for a count of four, hold your breath for a count of four (one bomb, two bomb, three bomb, four); exhale through your mouth for a count of four; hold your breath for a count of four (one bullet, two bullet, three bullet, four), and then restart the cycle.[103]

In this surreal 're-living'/re-embodiment of the moment-to-moment struggle of activists who have to fight by resisting and holding on to their breath, with carefully timed inhalations and exhalations, Sukkarieh makes us see 'combat breathing' not just as a source of violence but of resistance as well.

Pushing the limits of its epistemology into an even more performative register in her essay 'Unsewing My Lips, Breathing My Voice: The Spoken and Unspoken Truth of Transnational Violence' (2011), she envisions a surreal meeting with the spectre of 'transnational violence' whom she personifies as a zombie. Addressing 'it' directly, she learns that it is in the process of de-stressing by resorting to techniques of 'controlled breathing' or 'combat breathing', which it had learnt as part of its military training. In fact, it is so adept at this breathing that that it can function 'on auto pilot'.[104] Combat breathing, one could say, has become the habitus of transnational violence. Its discipline has enhanced the composure and self-control with which the agents of transnational violence can perfect the art of killing 'the walking dead and peace activists' with lethal strength. What Sukkarieh manages to complicate in the Fanonian narrative around 'combat

---

103 Omeima Sukkarieh, 'Unsewing my Lips: Breathing My Voice: The Spoken and Unspoken Truth of Transnational Violence', *Somatechnics* 1(1) (2011).
104 Sukkarieh, 'Unsewing my Lips'.

breathing' is that it can be used not just by activists but by perpetrators as well. While the activists believe that it provides them
with more stamina and a greater capacity to resist the actual
onslaught of bombs and bullets, the perpetrators believe that it
can be 'safe' for the world at large as a controlled way of killing.

As a footnote to this use of 'combat breathing' by the military
and police, one should remember that Yoga has been used from the
time of the Vietnam war as therapy by US soldiers fighting on
different battlefronts.[105] Today, even as its pedagogy in military
training has yet to be systematized, Yoga is increasingly recognized
as a 'holistic' therapy that is likely to 'make military personnel more
resilient'. One could question: Resilient in relation to countering
PTSD and pain management? Or in facilitating 'combat training'
as a means of developing 'better behaviour' in accepting the orders
of seniors in the military? Does the 'peace' induced by Yoga help
to calm the nerves or to kill more efficiently?

This militarist context of Yoga was pointed out to me by none
other than Chandralekha who, for all her devotion to the rigour of
Yoga in combating the violence of the world at artistic and
psychophysical levels, was nonetheless aware that Yoga can also be
used in negative ways, almost capitalizing on the necropolitical
use of controlled breathing to facilitate the death of others. One
may conclude from this insight that the transformative potential

---

105 For some perspectives on the use of Yoga in the US military and navy,
read Lindsay Tucker, 'How Yoga is Being Used Within the Military', *Yoga
Journal*, 27 September 2018: available at https://bityl.co/Aw7R; Stewart
J. Lawrence, 'Om in the Army, the US Military Gets Yoga', *The Guardian*,
31 August 2011: available at https://bityl.co/Aw7T. More recently, Indian and
US troops have carried out a bilateral army drill and joint training session
including Yoga at a training centre in Anchorage, Alaska. See 'Indian, US
Troops Carry Out Yoga Session, Joint Training Together in Alaska', *DNA*, 25
October 2021: available at https://bityl.co/Aw7Y.

of any psychophysical discipline whether it is dance or freediving or Yoga ultimately depends on the context and manner in which it is used. In this regard, one can invoke Wittgenstein when he reminded us that 'the meaning of a word lies in its use.' Likewise, the meaning of Yoga in all its fullness and spiritual vitality ultimately depends on its ethical practice.

* * *

Moving from the accounts of 'combat breathing' by Fanon and Sukkarieh to the condition of breathlessness during the pandemic, we know how a different kind of 'combat breathing' became inevitable for those patients in India who choked to death. Many of them failed to receive any oxygen in their final moments, a condition that can be attributed to a dereliction of duty by the State and the agencies of the health system which can be said to have monitored these cases of suffocation *by doing nothing about it.* Resolutely, they failed to act. Increasingly, of course, this inaction bordering on indifference has been accompanied by a belligerent denial on the part of the state and the medical industry of any lapse in their public duty and social services. Sadly, those who died in the process of being suffocated are already being forgotten in the public domain with no hope for legal compensation or redress. Amnesia has become the dominant symptom of our times in response to combat breathing.

In the United States, one encounters another history of combat breathing that continues to haunt public consciousness. I am referring to racist police brutality that has resulted in the forcible choking to death of African Americans and other minorities, whose dying words 'I can't breathe' can be regarded as the most searing epitaph of our times. While they have been most closely identified with the dying words of George Floyd, who is said to have repeated the word 'breathe' eleven times, even as a police officer pressed his knee against his neck for almost nine minutes, the same words have been uttered earlier by other victims of police brutality, notably Eric Garner, who was killed by a chokehold after being thrown to the ground. While there has been some judicial action against the assailants of these crimes, it has been legitimately criticized by supporters of the Black Lives Matter movement and other activist organizations as meagre and inadequate. What cannot be denied, however, is that there continues to be some kind of public memory of these racist crimes.

At a more personal level, the scary reflex of the words 'I can't breathe' gets echoed in our own daily interactions in the public sphere, where the suffocation of wearing a mask in hot and humid conditions on crowded streets as in my home city of Calcutta, makes one realize how the most extreme act of torture can be unconsciously recalled in more mundane symptoms of relatively mild physical discomfort. At such moments, we are alerted to the fact that we could be practising our own amateur version of combat breathing under the coercive protocols of social distancing and surveillance. Or, as Pugliese has put it graphically, our breathing has been 'occupied' to use Fanon's word, by the epidemiological directives of the state: 'wear the mask at all costs or risk contagion and death, even as the cluster of extreme environmental factors works to suffocate you.'[106] As this state of 'suffocation' becomes increasingly normalized, the words 'I can't breathe' have been systematically de-activated of any political association with police brutality and have come to be accepted as part of the deadly 'normalcy' of our times.

---

106 Correspondence with author, 5 October 2021.

Faced with these contradictions, we have a long way to go before we are in a position to fully confront the crisis of breathing in our times. Returning the discussion to the theatre, which has served as a vital point of reference in this narrative, almost like a shadow to the harsh reflections of death, grief, mourning and extinction, I would claim that if the pandemic has taught us anything at a performative level, it has been to complicate our far too euphoric and overly technical understanding of breath in the training of actors and their psychophysical resources. Ever since the theatres shut down across the world at the start of the pandemic in March 2020, with their claustrophobic interior spaces evoking repositories of contagion, we have become aware in an unprecedented way of the larger social and epidemiological dimensions of breathing. Earlier, we used to focus on actors breathing on stage to enunciate their lines, to throw their voices, to transform their physical presence, to sing with gusto, but we never really considered that we, the spectators in the audience, could be breathing as well. And not just breathing, but also coughing or clearing our throats, thereby affecting the air around us—and possibly infecting it—through inhalations and exhalations of invisible aerosols and droplets.

I cannot deny that a dimension of paranoia has crept into our awareness of public spaces from theatres and cinema halls to cafes and pubs, even as the semblance of normalcy seems to be returning with a vengeance to the cultures of everyday life in many parts of the world. Succumbing to paranoia, I would acknowledge, is as counter-productive as living in total defiance or wilful ignorance of the threat posed by the new viruses of our times. This is demonstrated by the growing number of anti-vaccination protestors, so self-righteously immersed in their dogmas of personal freedom that they fail to consider the rights of others. In this maelstrom of colliding attitudes, we need to strike a balance as we attempt to find a new 'movement in the pause', to return to Lepecki's arresting formulation, in order to arrive at a more resilient, level-headed, post-pandemic state of being.

With this in mind I would like to leave you with the last image in this narrative, which, on the surface, would seem to be the simplest and most rudimentary of asanas—the *savasana*. *Sava* means 'corpse'. This is the subtlest of all asanas because it requires a death-like stillness of being which can be animated only by the ever-renewing evanescence of infinitesimal breath. I bring up the savasana because the world in the last year has suffered a multitude of deaths, so multitudinous that I am reminded of one of the opening images of this narrative where I had called attention to hundreds of dead bodies embedded in the riverbanks of the Ganga. In these death-saturated times, it is curiously pertinent to remember the savasana, which testifies to the fact that breath is a source of rejuvenation in the living embodiment of a corpse. Between death and life, infection and rejuvenation, choking and hyperventilating, keeping our mouths shut and learning to inhale through the nose, we need to rethink how to breathe.

POSTSCRIPT

No end in sight, the pandemic continues, with the beginnings of the 'third wave' proliferating in some parts of the world and disappearing in others. As I bring this book to an end, I wish I could say that there is a sense of closure to the 'second wave'. Instead, one senses a deadly continuum as the third wave could well metamorphose into other strains of the virus. As it spread across the world, we faced a new 'variant of concern', strangely named Omicron, divested of the beginning letters 'nu' or 'xi' in the Greek alphabet which one might have expected from the protocols determining the nomenclature of new variants.[1] 'Nu', according to the World Health Organization, sounded too much like 'new', and 'xi', it explained, was too close to many last names to be found in China, notably that of the president of the People's Republic of China, Xi Jinping. Naming the new virus 'xi' might have been too politically undiplomatic, with President Xi being inevitably identified with the virus itself.

Literally meaning 'small o' and marked as the fifteenth letter in the Greek alphabet, Omicron (with the big 'O') was first identified in South Africa, even as it may not have originated there. More emphatically, it travelled with lightning speed, landing up, almost simultaneously, in diverse parts of the world, cutting across time zones and geographical regions. Once again, the virus in its

---

1 Jheelum Basu, 'Omicron: Why WHO Skipped "Xi" while Naming New Covid-19 Variant', *Outlook*, 28 November 2021. Available at https://bityl.co/ Aw7c

latest avatar demonstrated that it had no limits; it was cosmo-politan with a vengeance. The sheer speed of its transmission chal-lenged the premises of dromology in its instantaneous omni-presence of being here, there and everywhere. Nothing to be too perturbed about, as most epidemiologists seemed to concur, this virus had the mildest of symptoms, even as it could not prevent deaths from happening in the most mysterious of circumstances.

And so, as it became increasingly clear that the superspreader virus travelled most effectively on planes, penetrating inter-national borders with an insouciant wit, there was a moratorium on holiday plans to bring in the cheer of happy days with the antic-ipation of the New Year around the corner. As the New Year inau-gurated the 'third wave', the very sound of 'happy days' made one flinch with horror, reminding those of us living in India of our prime minister's erstwhile electoral slogan 'Achhe din aane waale hain' (Good days are coming). We have given up waiting for these acche din, and many have died cruel deaths in the process.

Maybe it is time to turn to Beckett's dark and wondrous play Happy Days where we see a middle-aged woman called Winnie prattling about the everydayness of life, preoccupying herself with seemingly insignificant daily actions like brushing her teeth and applying make-up and lipstick, while being incarcerated in a mound of earth which is her terrestrial home. In the first act, she is up to her waist in mud; in the second, she is up to her neck. And yet, with her head bobbing cheerfully, she continues to prattle, and in one throwaway line directed at her husband Willie, a more or less silent, invisible presence behind the mound of earth, who makes many failed attempts to slither into his hole like a slug, she declares: 'What a curse, mobility!'

I realize that I have cautioned the reader in the earlier section of this narrative against interpreting Beckett too strenuously within the temper of our times. Even so, taken out of context, this line resonates and provokes, not least because it cannot be pinned down to a single meaning. Can a character incarcerated in mud cursing mobility be taken too seriously? But can we (humans) in our craving for mobility and a total capitulation to its pleasures and desires—and to hell with global warming and climate change and the depletion of renewable energy resources—be taken seriously?

If this postscript seems far too cryptic, I would ask: Can there be weighty conclusions in such a state of deep uncertainty? Heraclitus would laugh. Better to introspect and learn to breathe more mindfully. Begin the care of the self with a deeper regard for the world and, more critically, a renewed respect for the planetary resources that we pillage and misuse so gratuitously for short-term gains.

In this wake-up call for our very existence, the pandemic can be regarded as a gift. But are we ready to accept it? Can we act on it? Can we learn to *unlearn* our habitual practices and imagined modes of expertise, and in the process, acquire a new humility? Steeped in suffering, Greek tragedies in the past nonetheless highlighted a painful moment of recognition, a critical 'opening of the eyes' (*anagnorisis*). Will we face the next wave with our eyes wide open, or shut?

BIBLIOGRAPHY

AGAMBEN, Giorgio. *Homo Sacer: Sovereign Power and Bare Life* (Daniel Heller-Roazen trans.). Stanford: Stanford University Press, 1998.

AIYAR, Swaminathan S. Anklesaria. 'How Rise of Low-Cost Guerrilla Media Aids Press Freedom'. *The Times of India*, 15 May 2022. Available at https://bit.ly/3yLvcLo

AJAY, Arkesh, and Aahana Dhar. 'To Honour Our Dead, We Must Remember the Horror of the COVID-19 Second Wave'. *The Caravan*, 6 June 2021. Available at https://bityl.co/Av73

AMIR, Fahim. 'A Touch Too Much: Animals of the Pandemic' in Ekaterina Degot and David Riff (eds), *There Is No Society? Individuals and Community in Pandemic Times*. Essen: Verlag der Buchandlung Walther Konig, 2020, pp. 157–73.

ARENDT, Hannah. *Eichmann in Jerusalem: A Report on the Banality of Evil*. New York: Penguin, 2006.

———. 'Preface: The Gap between Past and Future' in *Between Past and Future: Eight Exercises in Political Thought*. London: Penguin Classics, 2006, pp. 3–16.

ARNOLD, David. *Colonizing the Body: State Medicine and Epidemic Disease in Nineteenth Century India*. Berkeley and Los Angeles: University of California Press, 1993.

———. 'Death and the Modern Empire: The 1918–19 Influenza Epidemic in India'. *Transactions of the Royal Historical Society* 29 (2019): 181–200.

———. 'Pandemic India: Coronavirus and the Uses of History'. *Journal of Asian Studies* 79(3) (August 2020): 569–77.

ARTAUD, Antonin. 'The Theatre and the Plague' in *The Theatre and Its Double* (Mary Caroline Richards trans.). New York: Grove Press, 1958.

ASTON, Elaine. 'Caryl Churchill's "Dark Ecology"' in Carl Lavery and Clare Finburgh (eds), *Rethinking the Theatre of the Absurd: Ecology, the Environment, and the Greening of the Modern Stage*. London: Bloomsbury, 2015, pp. 59–76.

BARNES, Julian. *Levels of Life*. London: Jonathan Cape, 2013.

BARRY, John M. *The Great Influenza: The Story of the Deadliest Pandemic in History*. New York: Penguin, 2005.

BARTHES, Roland. *Camera Lucida: Reflections on Photography* (Richard Howard trans.). New York: Hill and Wang, 1981.

BASU, Jheelum. 'Omicron: Why WHO Skipped "Xi" while Naming New Covid-19 Variant'. *Outlook*, 28 November 2021. Available at https://bityl.co/Aw7c

BAXI, Upendra. 'Accelerating the "Avalanche of Evils": Towards Covid-19 Constitutionalism?' *India Legal*, 10 May 2021. Available at https://bityl.co/Av3o

BEARDSWORTH, Richard. *Derrida and the Political*. London and New York: Routledge, 1996.

BENJAMIN, Walter. 'The Author as Producer' in *Reflections: Essays, Aphorisms, Autobiographical Writings* (Edmund Jephcott trans., Peter Demetz ed.). New York: Schocken Books, 1986.

BERARDI, Franco. AND: *Phenomenology of the End*. Cambridge, MA: Semiotext(e)/Foreign Agents, 2015.

———. *Breathing: Chaos and Poetry*. Cambridge, MA: Semiotext(e) intervention series 26, 2019.

BERGER, John and Jean Mohr. *A Seventh Man: The Story of a Migrant Worker in Europe*. Cambridge: Granta Books, 1989 [1975].

BHABHA, Homi K. *The Location of Culture*. London: Routledge, 1994.

BHARUCHA, Rustom. *Chandralekha: Woman/Dance/Resistance*. New Delhi: HarperCollins, 1995.

———. 'Contextualizing Utopias: Reflections on Re-mapping the Present'. *Theater* 26(1–2) (1995): 32–49.

————. *Rajasthan: An Oral History; Conversations with Komal Kothari*. New Delhi: Penguin, 2003.

————. *Another Asia: Rabindranath Tagore and Okakura Tenshin*. New Delhi: Oxford University Press, 2006.

————. 'Countering Terror? The Search for Justice through Truth and Reconciliation' in *Terror and Performance*. London: Routledge, 2014, pp. 122–47.

————. 'Ravana as Dissident Artist' in Paula Richman and Rustom Bharucha (eds), *Performing the Ramayana Tradition: Enactments, Interpretations, and Arguments*. New York: Oxford University Press, 2021, pp. 142–57.

BILIMORIA, Purushottama. 'Hindu Response to Dying and Death in the Time of COVID-19'. *Frontiers in Psychology* 12 (2021). Available at https://bityl.co/Av9b

BIRKETT, Richard. 'A Politics of Memory: On Adrian Paci's "Interregnum"' (2017). *Mousse Magazine*, 1 October 2021. Available at https://bityl.co/AvAY

BOYCE, Mary. *Zoroastrians: Their Religious Beliefs and Practices*. London: Routledge, 2000.

BUTLER, Judith. *Antigone's Claim: Kinship between Life and Death*. New York: Columbia University Press, 2000.

————. *Precarious Life: The Powers of Mourning and Violence*. London: Verso, 2004.

————. *Frames of War: When Is Life Grievable?* London: Verso, 2010.

CECCO, Leyland. ' "Heat Dome" Probably Killed 1 BN Marine Animals on Canada Coast, Experts Say'. *The Guardian*, 8 July 2021. Available at https://bityl.co/AvzL

CHAKRABARTY, Dipesh. *The Climate of History in a Planetary Age*. Chicago: University of Chicago Press, 2021.

CHAKRABORTY, Aratrika and Anuradha Parihar. 'A Techno Legal Analysis of Admissibility of Digital Photographs as Evidence and Challenges'. *International Journal of Law* 3(5) (2017): 13–18.

CHAKRAVARTHI, Indira, and Imrana Qadeer. 'Covid-19: Reinforcing the "Technical Fix" and Distorting Public Health in India'. *Economic and Political Weekly* 56(51) (18 December 2021): 13–17.

CHANDRALEKHA. 'Who Are These Age-Old Female Figures?' *The Wire*, 8 March 2018. Available at https://bityl.co/B4Wy

CHATTERJEE, Partha. *Lineages of Political Society: Studies in Postcolonial Democracy*. New York: Columbia University Press, 2011.

CHOUDHARI, Ranjana. 'COVID 19 Pandemic: Mental Health Challenges of Internal Migrant Workers of India'. *Asian Journal of Psychiatry* 54 (December 2020). Available at https://bityl.co/Av8e

CHOUDHURY, Soumyabrata. *Now It's Come to Distances: Notes on Shaheen Bagh and Coronavirus, Association and Isolation*. New Delhi: Navayana, 2020.

CHURCHILL, Caryl. 'Not Not Not Not Not Enough Oxygen' in *Shorts*. London: Nick Hern Books, 2008.

CLARE, Stephanie. 'Geopower: The Politics of Life and Land in Frantz Fanon's Writing'. *Diacritics* 41(4) (2013): 60–80.

CLEWELL, Tammy. 'Mourning Beyond Melancholia: Freud's Psycho-analysis of Loss'. *Journal of the American Psychoanalytic Association* 52(1) (2004): 43–67.

COOLS, Guy. *Performing Mourning: Laments in Contemporary Art*. Amsterdam: Valiz, Antennae-Arts in Society, 2021.

COSGROVE, Ben. 'The Photo That Changed the Face of AIDS'. *Time*, 25 November 2014. Available at https://bityl.co/Av20

CROCKER, Lizzie. 'How Taryn Simon Created a Global Language of Grief'. *Daily Beast*, 13 April 2017. Available at https://bityl.co/AvAp

DANOWSKI, Déborah, and Eduardo Viveiros de Castro. *The Ends of the World* (Rodrigo Nunes trans.). Cambridge: Polity, 2016.

DAS, Veena. *Life and Words: Violence and the Descent into the Ordinary*. Berkeley and Los Angeles: University of California Press, 2007.

DEBORD, Guy. *The Society of the Spectacle* (Donald Nicholson-Smith trans.). New York: Zone Books, 1995.

DERRIDA, Jacques. 'Autoimmunity: Real and Symbolic Suicides' in Giovanna Borradori (ed.), *Philosophy in a Time of Terror: Dialogues with Jürgen Habermas and Jacques Derrida*. Chicago: University of Chicago Press, 2003.

DEVI, Mahasweta. *Rudali: From Fiction to Performance* (Anjum Katyal trans. and introd.). Calcutta: Seagull Books, 2007 [1997].

DNA. 'Indian, US Troops Carry Out Yoga Session, Joint Training Together in Alaska', 25 October 2021. Available at https://bityl.co/Aw7Y

DOYLE, Jennifer. *Hold It Against Me: Difficulty and Emotion in Contemporary Art*. Durham, NC: Duke University Press, 2013.

DUTT, Anonna. '20 Patients Die at Delhi's Jaipur Golden Hospital Due to Oxygen Shortage'. *The Hindustan Times*, 24 April 2021. Available at https://bityl.co/Ausz

ELLIS-PETERSEN, Hannah.' "The System Has Collapsed": India's Descent into Covid Hell'. *The Guardian*, 21 April 2021. Available at https://bityl.co/Autd

FANON, Frantz. *A Dying Colonialism* (Haakon Chevalier trans.). Ringwood: Pelican, 1970.

———. *The Wretched of the Earth* (Richard Philcox trans.). New York: Grove Press, 2005.

GHOSH, Amitav. *The Nutmeg's Curse: Parables for a Planet in Crisis*. New Delhi: Penguin, 2021.

GHOSH, Arjun. *Nabanna, Of Famine and Resilience: A Play*. New Delhi: Rupa, 2019.

GOLDMAN, Robert A. 'The Serpent and the Rope on Stage: Popular, Literary, and Philosophical Representations of Reality in Traditional India'. *Journal of Indian Philosophy* 14 (1986): 349–69.

———. 'Ā Garbhāt: Murderous Rage and Collective Punishment as Thematic Elements in Vyāsa's *Mahābhārata*' in Nell Shapiro Hawley and Sohini Sarah Pillai (eds), *Many Mahābhāratas*. Albany: SUNY Press, 2022, pp. 37–52.

GODREJ, Pheroza J., and Firoza Punthakey Mistree (eds). A *Zoroastrian Tapestry: Art, Religion, and Culture*. Ahmedabad: Mapin, 2002.

GORER, Geoffrey. *Death, Grief, and Mourning*. New York: Arno Press, 1977.

GOUDANA, Sozita. *Beckett's Breath: Anti-theatricality and the Visual Arts*. Edinburgh: Edinburgh University Press, 2018.

GUATTARI, Félix, and Gilles Deleuze. *Kafka: Toward a Minor Literature* (Dana Polan trans.). Minneapolis: University of Minnesota Press, 1986.

———. *A Thousand Plateaus: Capitalism and Schizophrenia*. Minneapolis: University of Minnesota Press, 1987.

Hindu (PTI). 'Coronavirus Lockdown: Image of a Weeping Rampukar Pandit Becomes Symbol of India's Migrant Worker Tragedy', 17 May 2020. Available at: https://bityl.co/Av8l

Hindu (Special Correspondent). 'Coronavirus: Aim Is to Win the War against COVID-19 in 21 Days, Says Narendra Modi', 25 March 2020. Available at: https://bityl.co/AutQ

Hindu (Staff Reporter). 1 May 2021, 'Oxygen Shortage: 12 Lives Lost in Delhi's Batra Hospital'. Available at https://bityl.co/Aut7

Hindustan Times (HT Correspondent). 'Parsis May Become Extinct By 2070?', 17 April 2006. Available at https://bityl.co/AwoO

HORN, Eva. *The Future as Catastrophe: Imagining Disaster in the Modern Age*. New York: Columbia University Press, 2018.

HYUNJUNG CHO. 'Hiroshima Peace Memorial Park and the Making of Japanese Postwar Architecture'. *Journal of Architectural Education* 66(1) (4 December 2012): 72–83.

THE INDIA FORUM. *India and the Pandemic: The First Year*. Hyderabad: Orient Blackswan, 2021.

Indian Express. 'Man, Who Sang for His Dying Mother, Sings Again in Tribute; Video Leaves People Emotional', 19 May 2021. Available at: https://bityl.co/AvyF

———. 'Son Sings "Tera Mujhse Hai" on Last Call to Woman Dying of Covid-19, Heartbroken Netizens Say "This Shouldn't Happen to Anyone"', 14 May 2021. Available at https://bityl.co/ AvyC

IYENGAR, B. K. S. *Light on Yoga*. London: Unwin Paperbacks, 1989.

JOBEY, Liz. 'Photographer Susan Meiselas: "Why Am I Making This Picture?"' *The Guardian*, 12 December 2008. Available at https://bityl.co/Autx

JOSHI, Aparna. 'COVID-19 Pandemic in India: Through Psycho-social Lens'. *Journal of Social and Economic Development* 23(Suppl. 2) (2021): 414–37. Available at https://bityl.co/Av7I

KAKAR, Sudhir. *Shamans, Mystics and Doctors: A Psychological Inquiry into India and Its Healing Traditions*. New Delhi: Oxford University Press, 2012 [1982].

KARVE, Iravati. *Yuganta: The End of an Epoch*. New Delhi: Sangam Books, 1974.

KAUR, G. B. 'Female Foeticide: A Danger to Society'. *Nursing Journal of India* 87(4) (April 1996): 77–8. Available at https://bityl.co/Avzo

KEENAN, Thomas and Eyal Weizman. *Mengele's Skull: The Advent of a Forensic Aesthetics*. Berlin: Sternberg Press, 2012.

KOPENAWA, Davi, and Bruce Albert. *The Falling Sky: Words of a Yanomami Shaman* (Nicholas Elliott and Alison Dundy trans). Cambridge, MA: Belknap Press, 2013.

LAKHANI, Somya, and Tora Agarwala. 'How COVID-19 Replaced Rituals of Mourning with a Solitary Grief'. *The Indian Express*, 16 August 2020. Available at https://bityl.co/Av6y

LAL, Vinay. *The Fury of Covid-19: The Politics, Histories, and Unrequited Love of the Coronavirus*. New Delhi: Macmillan, 2020.

LAWRENCE, Stewart J. 'Om in the Army, the US Military Gets Yoga'. *The Guardian*, 31 August 2011. Available at https://bityl.co/Aw7T

MADISON, Benjamin V. III. 'Seeing Can Be Deceiving: Photographic Evidence in a Visual Age—How Much Weight Does It Deserve?' *William and Mary Law Review* 25(4) (May 1984): 705–42. Available at https://bityl.co/BdFy

MANDER, Harsh. 'One Thing Was Distinctly Rotten about 2002 Gujarat Riots: Use of Rape as a Form of Terror'. *The Print*, 24 April 2019. Available at https://bityl.co/AvzE

———. *Locking Down the Poor: The Pandemic and India's Moral Centre*. New Delhi: Speaking Tiger, 2020.

MANOHARAN, Karthick Ram. *Frantz Fanon: Identity and Resistance*. New Delhi: Orient Blackswan, 2019.

MARLAND, Nickie. 'Roland Barthes: Camera Lucida—Lecture 10', 28 March 2017. *Photography Theory*. Available at https://bityl.co./AutH

MASHAL, Mujib, Sameer Yasir, and Shalini Venugopal Bhagat. 'At India's Funeral Pyres, Covid Sunders the Rites of Grief'. *The New York Times*, 8 May 2021. Available at https://bityl.co/Av3U

MBEMBE, Achille. 'Thoughts on the Planetary: An Interview with Achille Mbembe'. *New Frame*, 21 September 2019. Available at https://-bityl.co/Aw15

MCKENZIE, Jon. *Perform or Else: From Discipline to Performance*. London and New York: Routledge, 2001.

MEHTA, Tarini. 'Will We Ever Get Over the Grief of the Second Wave?' *India Today*, 25 June 2021.

MEISELAS, Susan. *Kurdistan: In the Shadow of History*. New York: Random House, 1997.

MENENDEZ, Bob, and Susan Collins. 'There Will Be Another Pandemic: Are We Prepared for It?' *The New York Times*, 14 June 2021. Available at https://bityl.co/Av2t

MENON, Ritu. *Address Book: A Publishing Memoir in the Time of Covid*. New Delhi: Women Unlimited, 2021.

MISHRA, Samina. *Jamlo Walks: An Illustrated Book about Life During Lockdown* (Tarique Aziz illus.). New Delhi: Puffin Books, 2021.

NAIR, Vasundharaa S., and Debanjan Banerjee. 'The Heterogeneity of Grief in India during Coronavirus Disease 2019 (COVID-19) and the National Lockdown'. *Asian Journal of Psychiatry* 54 (online edition, December 2020). Available at https://bityl.co/Av8R

NAQVI, Farah, Ruth Manorama, Malini Ghose, Sheba George, Syeda Hameed, and Mari Thekaekara. 'The Survivors Speak'. *Outlook*, 2 May 2002. Available at https://bityl.co/AvzI

NARAIN, Sunita (ed.). *The Pandemic Journal*. New Delhi: Centre for Science and Environment, 2021.

NIYOGI, Subhro. 'Son Sings to Dying Mother: Tera mujhse hai pehle ka naata koi'. *The Times of India*, 14 May 2021. Available at https://-bityl.co /AvyJ

PANDEY, Roli, Shilpi Kukreja and Kumar Ravi Priya. 'COVID-19: Mental Healthcare without Social Justice?' *Economic and Political Weekly* 55(31) (1 August 2020): 16–20.

PATEL, Vikram, Pamela Y. Collins, John Copeland, Ritsuko Kakuma, Sylvester Katontoka, Jagannath Lamichhane, Smita Naik, and Sarah Skeen. 'The Movement for Global Mental Health'. *British Journal of Psychiatry* 198(2) (February 2011): 88–90.

PHELAN, Peggy. *Unmarked: The Politics of Performance*. London and New York: Routledge, 1993.

———. *Mourning Sex: Performing Public Memories*. London and New York: Routledge, 1997.

PILLAI, Madhavankutty. 'The Virus That Killed 18 Million Indians'. *Open Magazine*, 6 September 2018. Available at https://bityl.co/Awoh

PUGLIESE, Joseph. *State Violence and the Execution of Law: Biopolitical Caesurae of Torture, Black Sites and Drones*. London and New York: Routledge, 2013.

———. *Biopolitics of the More-Than-Human: Forensic Ecologies of Violence*. Durham, NC: Duke University Press 2020.

RABILLARD, Sheila. 'On Caryl Churchill's Ecological Drama: Right to Poison the Wasps?' in Elaine Aston and Elin Diamond (eds), *The Cambridge Companion to Caryl Churchill*. Cambridge: Cambridge University Press, 2009, pp. 88–104.

RANA, Chahat. 'Citizens Collect Data as Government Obscures Oxygen Shortage Deaths Based on Technicalities'. *The Caravan*, 6 August 2021. Available at https://bityl.co/Ausq

RAU, Milo, in conversation with Achille Mbembe. 'The Paranoia of the Western Mind' in Ekaterina Degot and David Riff (eds), *There Is No*

Society? Individuals and Community in Pandemic Times. Essen: Verlag der Buchandlung Walther Konig, 2020, pp. 125–37.

ROBERTS, Jillian. 'What Happens When a Loved One Dies?: Our First Talk About Death' (Cindy Revell illus.). No. 2 in the 'Just Enough' Series. Victoria, Canada: Orca Book Publishers, 2016.

ROSE, Deborah Bird. 'In the Shadow of All This Death' in Jay Johnston and Fiona Probyn-Rapsey (eds), *Animal Death.* Sydney: Sydney University Press, 2013, pp. 1–20.

———, Thom van Dooren, and Matthew Chrulew. 'Introduction: Telling Extinction Stories' in Deborah Bird Rose, Thom van Dooren and Matthew Chrulew (eds), *Extinction Studies: Stories of Time, Death, and Generations* (New York: Columbia University Press, 2017), pp. 1–18.

ROY, Arundhati. ' "We Are Witnessing a Crime against Humanity": Arundhati Roy on India's Covid Catastrophe'. *The Guardian,* 28 April 2021. Available at https://bityl. co/AutE

SATCHIDANANDAN, K., and Nishi Chawla (eds). *Singing in the Dark: A Global Anthology of Poetry under Lockdown.* New Delhi: Vintage Books, 2020.

SAX, William, and Claudia Lang. *The Movement for Global Mental Health: Critical Views from South and Southeast Asia.* Amsterdam: Amsterdam University Press, 2021.

SCHECHNER, Richard. *Performative Circumstances: From the Avant-Garde to the Ramlila.* Calcutta: Seagull Books, 1983.

SEARLE, Adrian. 'Taryn Simon: *An Occupation of Loss* Review—Transfixing Cacophony from a Secret Underworld'. *The Guardian* (18 April 2018). Available at https://bityl.co/AvAy

SEKULA, Allan. 'Dismantling Modernism, Reinventing Documentary: Notes on the Politics of Representation'. *Massachusetts Review* 19(4) (Winter 1978): 859–83.

———. 'The Traffic in Photographs'. *Art Journal* 41(1) (Photography and the Scholar/Critic special issue) (Spring 1981): 15 –25. Available at https://bityl.co/BdFf

———. 'Photography and the Limits of National Identity'. *Grey Room* 55 (2014): 28–33. Available at https://bityl.co/BIFN

———. 'On the Invention of Photographic Meaning' in *Photography Against the Grain: Essays and Photo Works, 1973–1983*. London: MACK Books, 2016.

SEN, Amartya. *Poverty and Famines: An Essay on Entitlement and Deprivation*. Oxford: Clarendon Press, 1981.

———. 'More Than 100 Million Women Are Missing'. *The New York Review of Books*, 20 December 1990. Available at https://bityl.co/ Avz8

SENGUPTA, Shuddhabrata. 'Kumbh 2021: Astrology, Mortality, and the Indifference to Life of Leaders and Stars'. *The Wire*, 20 April 2021. Available at: https://bityl.co/Bavs

SHAH, Sonia. *Pandemic*. New Delhi: HarperCollins, 2020.

SHERWELL, Philip. 'Modi Leads India into Viral Apocalypse'. *The Australian*, 25 April 2021. Available at https://bityl.co/AutY

SHULMAN, David. *Dark Hope: Working for Peace in Israel and Palestine*. Chicago and London: University of Chicago Press, 2007.

———. *More Than Real: A History of the Imagination in South India*. Cambridge, MA: Harvard University Press, 2012.

SILBEY, Jessica. 'Images in/of Law'. *New York Law School Law Review* 57: 171–83.

SINGH, Bandeep. '90 Km with Migrant Hope: Capturing Exodus of Migrant Workers in 13 Stills'. *India Today*, 15 April 2020. Available at https:/bityl.co/Auuq

SMOLAK, Anna. 'People of No Consequence by Aslan Gaisumov' (October 2016) at Mezosfera.org. Available at https://bityl.co/AvAd

SONTAG, Susan. *On Photography*. New York: Anchor Books / Doubleday, 1977.

———. *Regarding the Pain of Others*. New York: Farrar, Straus and Giroux, 2003.

SPINNEY, Laura. *Pale Rider: The Spanish Flu of 1918 and How It Changed the World*. London: Vintage, 2018.

———. 'Vital Statistics: How the Spanish Flu of 1918 Changed India'. *The Caravan*, 19 October 2018. Available at https://bityl.co/Auuo

SUKKARIEH, Omeima. 'Unsewing my Lips: Breathing My Voice: the Spoken and Unspoken Truth of Transnational Violence'. *Somatechnics* 1(1) (2011): 124–33.

THAKUR, Purusottam, and Kamlesh Painkra. 'Jamlo's Last Journey along a Locked-Down Road'. People's Archive of Rural India (PARI), 14 May 2020. Available at https://bityl.co/BavX

THAPAR, Romila. *Time as a Metaphor of History*. New Delhi: Oxford University Press, 1996.

Times of India. 'BTS Deliver Powerful Speech on Climate Change, Importance of Covid Vaccine and Hope for the Future at UNGA; Say "Every Choice We Make Is the Beginning of Change"', 20 September 2021. Available at https://bityl.co/BdLM

———. 'WHO Says Millions of Covid Deaths Went Unreported in India; Centre Questions Methodology', 5 May 2022. Available at https://bit.ly/3lj2d9L

TRUBRIDGE, William. *Oxygen: A Memoir*. New Zealand: HarperCollins, 2017.

TUCKER, Lindsay. 'How Yoga Is Being Used Within the Military'. *Yoga Journal*, 27 September 2018. Available at https://bityl.co/Aw7R

TUMBE, Chinmay. *The Age of Pandemics 1817–1920: How They Shaped India and the World*. New Delhi: HarperCollins, 2020.

VARADARAJAN, Siddharth. *Gujarat: The Making of a Tragedy*. New Delhi: Penguin, 2002.

VERMA, Abhinav, and Radhika Roy. 'Why India Needs to Set Up a Truth Commission to Help It Really Heal from the Covid-19 Pandemic'. *Scroll.in*, 8 March 2022. Available at https://bityl.co/Av2l

VERMA, Gargi. '12-Year-Old Walks 100 Km, Dies Just Short of Bijapur Home'. *The Indian Express*, 21 April 2020. Available at https://bityl.co/Av1m

VIRILIO, Paul. *Speed and Politics: An Essay on Dromology* (Mark Pollizzotti trans.). New York: Semiotext[e], 1986.

WAKELING, Corey. *Beckett's Laboratory: Experiments in the Theatre Enclosure*. London: Methuen Drama, 2021.

WEBB, Holly. 'Top 10 Children's Books on Death and Bereavement'. *The Guardian*, 5 February 2015. Available at: https://bityl.co/Bavc

WOLFE, Cary. 'Foreword' in Deborah Bird Rose, Thom van Dooren and Matthew Chrulew (eds), *Extinction Studies: Stories of Time, Death, and Generations*. New York: Columbia University Press, 2017, pp. *vii–xvi*.

ZHANG, Michael. 'Corbis Images Sold By Bill Gates To Visual China Group'. *PetaPixel* 22 (January 2016). Available at: https://bityl.co/BdEL

PHOTO CREDITS

Page 8 Patients suffering from Covid-19 get treatment at the casualty ward in Lok Nayak Jai Prakash Hospital, amidst the spread of the disease in New Delhi (15 April 2021). Photograph by Danish Siddiqui. Image © Reuters [RTXBI71K]

Page 14 A man runs past the burning funeral pyres of those who died from the coronavirus during a mass cremation, at a crematorium in New Delhi (26 April 2021). Photograph by Adnan Abidi. Image © Reuters [RTXBT8G9]

Page 18 Relatives carry a body for cremation past the Ganga where bodies were dumped during the pandemic. Photograph by Ritesh Shukla. Image © Getty Images News [GettyImages-1319087966]

Pages 42, 43 and 44 Migrant exodus (15 April 2020). Photographs by Bandeep Singh. Images courtesy Bandeep Singh and *India Today*.

Page 75 Rampukar Pandit (17 May 2020). Photograph by Atul Yadav. Image © Press Trust of India (PTI) [PTI11-05-2020_000225A]

Page 116 Maya Krishna Rao, performing *Walk* at Jantar Mantar, New Delhi, 22 January 2013. Screenshot from YouTube. Reproduced with permission from the artist.

Page 175 Portrait of Chandralekha. Photograph by Sadanand Menon. Image courtesy The Chandralekha Archive, SPACES, Chennai.

Page 182 William Trubridge diving. Photograph by Louisa Jane. Image courtesy William Trubridge, *Oxygen: A Memoir*.

ACKNOWLEDGEMENTS

I would like to thank my publisher Naveen Kishore of Seagull Books in my home city of Calcutta for responding so empathetically to my manuscript as it was in the process of being completed in the last months of the 'second wave'. He realized the urgency of a prompt publication for which I am grateful. Sunandini Banerjee, Senior Editor at Seagull Books, who is also their designer, engaged with my manuscript with vibrant energy and an attention to detail. I am also grateful to Bishan Samaddar for his careful supervision of the logistics and production. At a time when publishing a book has become an increasingly mechanical and anonymous process, when one almost never gets to meet the editorial or production team, I have to acknowledge that it has been a pleasure to interact with the entire team of Seagull Books at their creative hub in Calcutta, which is, after all, the city in which I lived through the pandemic.

I am grateful to a number of readers with whom I shared the manuscript as it was a work-in-progress—Stephen Barber, Paul Carter, Sadanand Menon, Jerry Pinto and Mohan Rao. Their suggestions and incisive comments have greatly contributed to the texturing of my revisions.

For the section on photography, I learned a lot from early conversations with professional photographers like Pablo Bartholomew, Navroze Contractor and Sondeep Shankar, and ongoing conversations with Christina Zueck, who introduced me to the work of Bandeep Singh, whose work features prominently in Chapter 1. I am grateful to Bandeep and India Today for allowing Seagull Books to reprint some of the images. I would also acknowledge PhotoSouthAsia for publishing a short intervention on photography during the pandemic in October 2021, which catalysed my more elaborate reflections on the subject in Chapter 1.

On legal issues relating to photography, I am grateful to Professor Upendra Baxi and Adil Hasan Khan for their valuable inputs and to Gautam Bhatia, Arvind Narrain and Oishik Sircar for some brief but useful conversations. I thank David Arnold for his clarifications relating to the history of epidemics and pandemics. For matters relating to public healthcare, I am grateful to William Sax for sharing a copy of his recent co-edited book on the movement for global mental health which has been enormously useful for my research. My friend Mohan Rao has been a constant provider of references for debates and controversies relating to Covid-19, the politics surrounding vaccines and the general indifference of the Indian government to public health.

On questions relating to grief and mourning, I am grateful to Sudhir Kakar for introducing me to Dr Amrita Narayanan who provided some useful insights in the early stages of my research. My long-term correspondent Rowena Hill has also shared some sharp perspectives on the poetics of mourning. I had a particularly productive exchange of views with dance dramaturg Guy Cools, who shared his book *Performing Mourning* at a time when I needed to read it. His reflections on mourning have contributed to Chapter 2, particularly in the section focusing on Euro-American representations of mourning through diverse art practices.

For the section dealing with extinction, climate change and global warming, I am indebted to an intimate but intellectually charged symposium on 'the ends', which was co-curated for Performance Studies international (PSi) by Felipe Cervera, Kyoko Iwaki, Eero Laine and Kristof van Baarle. The insights of this symposium provided the conceptual ground for Chapter 3. I am particularly grateful to Kristof for following up on the symposium with any number of inspiring publications that helped me to widen my perspective on matters relating to extinction and death. For some crucial clarifications on Frantz Fanon in relation to 'combat breathing' I am grateful to Joseph Pugliese for his penetrating analysis on the matter and to Karthick Ram Manoharan for his perspective.

I should add that even as libraries and archives were closed during the pandemic that I was able to access valuable research material on the

Internet and electronic library facilities. In this regard, I am grateful to Bhargav Rani and Sourav Roy who have facilitated my virtual retrieval of any number of valuable essays and books. André Lepecki also provided a much-needed weblink for his valuable research on 'movement in the pause' while Becky Britton Pillai enabled me to access some contemporary insights on children's picture books relating to death.

At a more personal level, I would like to acknowledge my circle of friends who enlivened the dark days of the pandemic with lively online conversations and creative dreaming. Some of these friends I have not yet met in person, notably Rodolfo García Vásquez from the Os Satyros theatre group in São Paulo, with whom much has been shared on a decolonial performance aesthetic via Zoom. Nearer home I have been in ceaseless conversation with performer Maya Krishna Rao whose incendiary production *Walk* figures prominently in the book, and Sadanand Menon who enabled me to re-live those extraordinary moments of watching Chandralekha's production of *Prana*, as it was in the process of evolving at the open-air Mandala theatre on Elliot's Beach in Chennai.

One of the most moving aspects of writing this book has been the opportunity to pay tribute to Chandralekha's 'homage to breath' in productions like *Prana*, which I juxtapose with the deep-sea freediving skills of world champion William Trubridge, whose aquatic sense of being-in-the-world also figures prominently in the last part of the narrative. My thanks to Sam Trubridge for making the connection with his brother whose aquatic research I first learnt about from writings relating to the decentralized *Fluid States* conference organized by PSi, one of whose locations was Dean's Blue Hole in the Bahamas.

I am grateful to all the contributors to this book.